The History of Ancient Egypt
Part I
Professor Robert Brier

THE TEACHING COMPANY ®

PUBLISHED BY:

THE TEACHING COMPANY
4151 Lafayette Center Drive, Suite 100
Chantilly, Virginia 20151-1232
1-800-TEACH-12
Fax—703-378-3819
www.teach12.com

ISBN 1-56585-622-8

Robert Brier, Ph.D.

Long Island University

Bob Brier was born in the Bronx, where he still lives. He received his bachelor's degree from Hunter College and Ph.D. in philosophy from the University of North Carolina at Chapel Hill in 1970.

From 1981–1996 he was Chairman of the Philosophy Department at C.W. Post campus of Long Island University and now primarily teaches Egyptology courses. He was Director of the National Endowment for the Humanities' Egyptology Today Program and has twice been selected as a Fulbright Scholar. He is also the recipient of the David Newton Award for Teaching Excellence.

In 1994, Dr. Brier became the first person in 2,000 years to mummify a human cadaver in the ancient Egyptian style. This research was the subject of a National Geographic television special, *Mr. Mummy*. Dr. Brier is also the host of The Learning Channel's series *The Great Egyptians*.

Professor Brier is the author of *Ancient Egyptian Magic* (Morrow: 1980), *Egyptian Mummies* (Morrow: 1994), *Encyclopedia of Mummies* (Facts on File: 1998), *The Murder of Tutankhamen: A True Story* (Putnam's: 1998), *Daily Life in Ancient Egypt* (Greenwood: 1999), and numerous scholarly articles.

Table of Contents
The History of Ancient Egypt
Part I

The History of Ancient Egypt

Scope:

There is something about ancient Egypt that fascinates almost everyone. Egyptian exhibits at museums draw the largest crowds, mummy movies pull in the largest audiences, and Egypt attracts the most tourists. Part of the attraction is undoubtedly the exotic nature of the beast. Treasures hidden in tombs seem always just around the corner; hieroglyphs, while beautiful, seem impossible to read; and the beautiful sculptures and paintings seem from a time incredibly long ago. In a sense, one goal of this course is to demystify ancient Egypt but not to take the fun out of it.

As we learn more and more about Egypt, it will all become familiar. Students will have an idea of how hieroglyphs work and what they say; we will come to know how archaeologists, using scholarship and learning, search for undiscovered tombs; and we will learn the techniques used to create the art of ancient Egypt. But as we learn more and more, the student should become more and more amazed by the culture. What was created on the banks of the Nile was an event unique in human history. No civilization lasted so long, contributed so much, or repeatedly amazed as did ancient Egypt.

Because Egyptian history lasted so long, Egyptologists divide it into three periods called *Kingdoms*: (1) The Old Kingdom saw the beginnings of nationhood for Egypt under one supreme ruler, the pharaoh. During this period, the pyramids were built, and the rules of Egyptian art were established that would govern for 3,000 years. (2) The Middle Kingdom, a period of stabilizing after the Old Kingdom collapsed, saw a nation fighting to regain its greatness. (3) The New Kingdom, the glamour period of ancient Egypt, was when all the stars—Hatshepsut, Tutankhamen, Ramses the Great, and others—appeared.

We will chronologically survey the full 3,000 years of recorded ancient Egyptian history, emphasizing that the ancient Egyptians were people just like ourselves, motivated by the same fears, doubts, and hopes. By the end of the course, students should feel that they know the kings and queens who made Egypt great. As we study the different reigns, we will also discuss various aspects of Egyptian civilization so that you should learn far more than just the rulers of ancient Egypt. You should be able to walk through the Egyptian collection of a museum and tell when a statue was carved, have an idea which pharaoh it is by the way the face is carved, and perhaps even be able to read the hieroglyphs to discern the king's name. In short, I want to turn out "junior Egyptologists," people with a deep understanding of Egypt, for whom ancient artifacts will not all look the same.

To a great extent, the fun of history is in the details. Knowing what kind of wine Tutankhamen preferred makes him come alive. Knowing that Ramses the Great was crippled by arthritis for the last decade of his long life makes us more sympathetic to the boastful monarch who fathered more than one hundred children. If we understand what it was like to be a miner sent to the turquoise mines in the Sinai in the summer, we will feel a kinship with our long dead counterparts. As we wind our way chronologically through thirty centuries of history, we will pause repeatedly to look at the details that make up the big picture.

The first five lectures will really be a prolegomena. We will see what Egypt was like before writing, and we will learn how Egyptologists piece together the history of ancient Egypt. We will see how we know what we know—how hieroglyphs were deciphered, for example—and we will see that since then, Egyptology has been one ongoing detective story.

In Lectures Six through Ten, we will see the Egyptians rise to a greatness far surpassing any other people in the Near East. We learn of a king who united Egypt by might and of a pharaoh who showed Egypt how to build the pyramids. While we see how the pyramids were built, we will learn just what it was that made Egypt great. At the end of these lectures, we will see Egypt collapse into a dark age about which little is known, and we will try to figure out what happened.

Lectures Eleven through Sixteen discuss Egypt's successful attempt to pull itself together, only to collapse once again. We see heroic kings from the south battle to unite the country and establish a peace that would last for two centuries—as long as the United States has existed. Then we will see Egypt invaded by the mysterious people called the Hyksos, only to watch as the kings of the south battle Egypt back to greatness. We will also look in detail at the Old

Testament story of Joseph in Egypt to see what light it might shed on this period.

Lectures Seventeen through Twenty-Five deal with the fabulous Dynasty XVIII, the period of Egypt's greatest wealth and personalities. We will take in-depth looks at the kings and queens of this period. We will see Hatshepsut, the woman who ruled as king; Akhenaten, the first monotheist in history, who changed the religion of Egypt; and Tutankhamen, the son of Akhenaten, who became the most famous of Egypt's kings when his undisturbed tomb was discovered in 1922.

Lectures Twenty-Five through Twenty-Eight are a brief excursion into my specialty, mummies. We will talk about everything you ever wanted to know about mummies, including how to make one. We will also see that mummies are like books—packed with information—if you know how to read them.

Lectures Twenty-Nine through Thirty-Five focus on the end of the New Kingdom, the last great epoch of Egyptian history. Dominated by Ramses the Great, this period also had other important kings, and we will discuss who was the unnamed pharaoh of the Exodus.

In Lectures Thirty-Six through Forty-One, we will see Egypt's greatness slipping away. Egypt will be invaded by a series of conquering peoples, including Nubians, Libyans, and Persians. It is a sad story, and we will examine the causes of Egypt's decline.

Egypt's last gasp is under the Greek kings, the Ptolemies. This period begins with the conquest of Alexander the Great and ends with Cleopatra. For two hundred years, once mighty Egypt is ruled by kings named Ptolemy, all descended from General Ptolemy who served under Alexander. In Lectures Forty-Two through Forty-Seven, we will trace what life was like for an Egyptian under the oppressive rule of their Greek masters.

It is a long and fascinating history, but the study of Egypt should not end with this course. There will be suggestions of how to continue learning about Egypt—societies to join, events to attend, books to read. The adventure should not end here.

Lecture One
Introduction

Scope:

In this lecture, we will discuss five basic points: (1) why we should study ancient Egypt, (2) what the approaches of the course will be, (3) how we know what we know about Egypt, (4) how the course will be organized, and (5) the goals of the course—what I hope to achieve and what the student can expect from the forty-eight lectures.

Outline

I. Why should we study ancient Egypt? There is something very special about Egypt—it is an attractive escape from our everyday world.

    A. Egypt is the most advanced ancient civilization in history. Its accomplishments include monumental architecture (the pyramids), medical science, monotheism, and mummification.

    B. Even if the hieroglyphs are decipherable, Egypt remains one of the most mysterious civilizations in history.

    C. Finally, Egyptian art is among the most beautiful of all time.

II. There are various approaches to Egyptology.

    A. The philological approach—for example, that of Sir Alan Gardiner—studies the language.

    B. The historical approach looks at Egypt through events and documents, often in relation to Egypt's neighbors. This is my approach.

    C. The art historical approach looks at ancient Egypt through its art. Egyptian art maintains great continuity for 3,000 years, subscribing to eternal values rather than creativity and innovation.

III. Art and literature reveal much about this civilization.

    A. Tomb paintings tell us about the Egyptians' belief in the afterlife.

    B. Tombs were provisioned with an amazing variety of everyday objects.

    C. Temple walls give us histories, such as records of battles and lists of kings.

    D. We have religious texts on papyrus, wood, and stone. The Book of the Dead reveals what Egyptians thought about the next world.

    E. Literature, especially fiction and love poetry, gives us additional insight into the beliefs of the Egyptians.

    F. Herodotus, the Greek historian from the fifth century B.C., provides further observations of Egypt, even if they aren't always reliable.

IV. This course is based on the following method.

    A. We will emphasize people and their achievements in an effort to make the dead come alive.

    B. The course will be chronological, ending with Cleopatra, and will include a few detours along the way. One such detour will be my specialty, paleopathology.

    C. Dates will be minimally important—you're not going to remember them anyway. The relative chronology of events is what matters.

V. The course has several goals.

    A. The first goal is to gain an understanding of Egyptian history, architecture, religion, and mythology.

    B. The second goal is to increase your appreciation of the art of ancient Egypt.

    C. The final goal is to motivate you to continue learning after the course is over.

Lecture One—Transcript
Introduction

Hi, I'm Bob Brier and we're going to be together for 48 lectures, so I think it might be a good idea to convince you that you did the right thing. What I'm going to do this first lecture is try to explain to you why it's the right thing to study Egypt, why it's a good thing. But I'll also explain to you how we know what we know about Egypt. We know an incredible amount about Egypt. We don't know as much about say the Mayans, or the Assyrians, or the Babylonians, but we know lots about the Egyptians, and I'm going to explain why that is.

Another thing I'm going to explain is that there are different approaches to the subject. Different people approach Egyptology in different ways; they have different biases. I'll explain my bias also, and then I'm going to do some housekeeping. I'm going to tell you how the course is organized. I'm going to explain how we will be proceeding and what I expect of you. But also, I want to explain the goals. I want to tell you what I expect that you will get out of this course.

But let me start with why you should be learning Egyptology. Now first, let me say this, there is an element of escapism in it. Egypt is a wonderful place to go when you're tired of the real world, when things get too busy, when things are too hectic. Egypt is a place far, far away in time and space. I can give you an example, a personal example. About three years ago now, I had the schedule from hell. I was teaching five different courses at three different campuses and it was just crazy. Sometimes I literally didn't know where I was going. I was in the car thinking, "Now, which course am I teaching now, where am I going?" And to keep my sanity, in the afternoons when I would get back to my office, I would go there and for a half hour I would just draw hieroglyphs. I would draw a line of birds or a line of snakes or a line of feet, and it was a great escape and it helped.

There is a kind of psychological reason I think why people study Egypt. I mean, I find it in my students at the university. I'll often ask a kid who is an accounting major, "Why are you taking Egyptology?" And very often the kid will say, "You know, I take loads of accounting courses, loads of economics; this has absolutely no relevance to my life—to my career—and I love it." So there is a kind of psychological reason for doing it. So I think you'll enjoy it for that reason.

But there are better reasons, and let me tell you about some of those. Ancient Egypt was the most advanced civilization in the ancient world. Now there are some people who would disagree with that. The people who study Sumeria; for example, Samuel Noah Kramer was a great scholar on Sumeria and he wrote a book called *History Begins at Sumer* where he outlined all the things that begin in Sumeria. He was wrong; history does not begin at Sumeria. It really starts in Egypt, but that's a bit of my prejudice, but let me explain why Egypt is so special among the cultures of the ancient world.

There are so many firsts in Egypt that we all know about; that makes Egypt unique. For example, the Sumerians did not build the pyramids of Egypt. The Sumerians did not build the incredible temples we see. The Sumerians did not do medical science the way the Egyptians did. There are loads of firsts in ancient Egypt; that's why Egypt is important. For example, religion. Most people are shocked to learn that monotheism, the belief in one god, is first presented by an Egyptian pharaoh. Monotheism starts in Egypt. Or, for example, mummification. It's the Egyptians who perfected the science of mummification. Or Egyptian mythology. Nothing, no mythology is as rich as Egyptian mythology. I mean Egypt is incredible. For example, the Greeks, the famous Greeks, the ancient civilization, they revered ancient Egypt. If you read Greek historians, they all say the same thing: We got our civilization from Egypt. They wanted to trace their lineage back to the Egyptians, because the Greeks were sort of Johnny-come-latelys on the scene compared to the Egyptians. Here you're talking about *The Iliad*, *The Odyssey*, maybe being composed around 900 B.C. The pyramids were built a couple of thousand years earlier. So the Greeks always wanted to trace their—it's like, when people want to trace their heritage back to the Mayflower, "my ancestors came over on the Mayflower," that's what the Greeks did with Egypt. I mean, there is a wonderful story. When the Greeks were holding the Olympiad, they wanted to figure out how to make it fair, because there were foreigners who wanted to participate in the Olympiad, in the Olympic Games. They figured, well, we have Greek officials, how would we make it fair, they might be biased toward the Greeks. So they sent a committee to Egypt, because the Egyptians were wise in philosophy. And they asked the

Egyptians: How do we make it fair? So the Greeks really wanted to trace everything back to Egypt. I mean, there is nothing like Egypt.

Let me say another thing: If you ask the ancient Greeks where did you learn to build your temples they all said the same thing, "We learned to build in stone from the Egyptians." The first building in stone in the history of the world is an Egyptian building, but we'll talk about that later. So there are plenty of reasons for studying Egypt.

Another reason is, I think, that Egypt is somewhat mysterious. People look at the hieroglyphs, and they look indecipherable. They are not. One of the things I'm going to do with you, I hope, in these 48 lectures is demystify Egypt, but I don't think it will take any of the wonder away from it, any of the grandeur of Egypt. But I'm going to show you what those birds, and snakes, and ducks really mean. But there is this mysterious aspect about Egypt. I mean, this is why I think every person who thinks he is reincarnated thinks he was an ancient Egyptian. They were never a shoemaker in Brooklyn; they were always an ancient Egyptian. So I think that there is this mysterious aspect about Egypt that also draws us to it.

And then there is the art. There's nothing like Egyptian art. Think about it. If you go into a museum and you look at Greek art, and I'm not demeaning Greek art, it's wonderful, the wonderful kraters, the large pots, Cycladic idols are very stylistic, terrific. But it's just not Egyptian art. It's not that colorful, vibrant; there is something special about Egyptian art. And we'll talk about that later, too. So there are plenty of reasons why we should study Egypt, and that's why I think you're going to enjoy it.

But let me move on. Let me say that there are various approaches to how to study Egypt, and it's important that you understand these different approaches, because they are biases, and I have my bias and I'll talk about that. The first is what we call the philological approach. Now philological comes from two Greek words: *philo*, which is love, and *logos*, which is words. It's the love of words. Philologists are the language people; these are the translators. These are the guys who take a really tough text and can translate it. Now all of us, when I say us, I mean Egyptologists; we can all translate hieroglyphs moderately well. But when you get a really tough text, we go to the philologists. And there is an approach to the history Egypt that's philological, through the language. Sir Alan Gardiner, a great scholar of the 1930s, 1940s, was a philologist. His specialty was language, hieroglyphs. He wrote a history of Egypt. A solid history, lots of good stuff in it, but it's mainly through language. I'll give you an example of how you figure out the history of Egypt through language. Take one pharaoh's name, the pharaoh Montuhotep, made up of two Egyptian words. *Montu*, who is a war god. And *hotep* means "to be pleased." This is why you get lots of pharaohs whose names are things like Amenhotep, right, Montuhotep, so it means, "Montu the war god is pleased." Now as Sir Alan Gardiner points out, that tells you something about the times. Why name a kid Montuhotep? You know? It means there is war and you want to be in favor with the war god. So just from the name we can get an idea of the political times. So there is a philological approach mainly through texts and analyzing language of trying to figure out history, and it's a legitimate approach. It's not mine.

I'll tell you the one drawback. Alan Gardiner's book, it's very solid, as I said, lots of good information, but it's unreadable, I mean, it's deadly. And I always think when I look at Alan Gardiner's stuff, I always think of a man named Weigall. Arthur Weigall was the inspector of antiquities in the Valley of the Kings when Tutankhamen's tomb was discovered. And he's the best writer on archeology that you will find. In the preface to one of his books, Weigall says: "It's the goal of the archeology writer to make the dead come alive, not to put the living to sleep." And I think he's right.

This is why I have my approach. And let me explain what my approach is. In my approach to history I try to emphasize events and the people who made those events happen. We're going to go through Egyptian history learning events and the people involved. I think that's probably the best way to do it. There is just something about people that makes the past come alive, once we realize that these were not just abstract kings but real people with the same kind of emotions we have. Ramses the great one, when he went into battle he was afraid. Don't listen to what he put on his temple wall, he was probably afraid. So I think there are lots of different approaches, and I'm going to try to take the broadest approach.

But let me tell you one other approach that I think is also legitimate, the art historical approach. Now this is the approach that is usually taken by art historians, people who are specialists in the art of ancient Egypt. They are usually museum curators. These are the people who are happy in their museums and don't go to Egypt that much, they don't excavate, they are happy to have, say, the objects, the art brought to them. And then these are the people who can look at a fragment of a statue. They can look at, for example, the way the mouth curls downwards, just a little piece of statue, and say, "Ah, look at the way the corner has a drill mark. That didn't start until the late period, so we know that it's probably 750 B.C. or later." Or they can look at an eye, and just from the eyebrow, they can tell you roughly the period, maybe even the pharaoh. And many of these people, when they write their articles, it's reconstructing the history of Egypt through the art.

Now let me say something about the art, because it's amazing how central to Egyptian culture the art was. Let me try something out on you that I think you probably never thought about. When you go into a museum, a museum with a large collection of Egyptian art, and you look at an Egyptian statue, let's say it's of a pharaoh striding forward. If that statue was carved in 2500 B.C., you look at and you say, "Egyptian." You can look at a statue carved a thousand years later, 1500 B.C., and say the same thing, "Ah, that's Egyptian." And you go to one carved 500 B.C., "Ah, Egyptian." There's relatively little change. The art didn't change over 3,000 years. And that's a curious factor.

You can't do that with any other art. I mean, think about what's happened in Western art in the last 200 years. You go from Picasso to this to that—I mean from a Madonna and child to the Middle Ages, I mean, it's crazy. But Egyptian art never changed, at least not the broad picture. And let me explain why, why the art historians think what they do is the most important.

Egyptian art wasn't supposed to change. They didn't value creativity. The Egyptians did not want innovations. When you carved a statue you were supposed to carve it for eternity. It was supposed to be the way we've been carving it for hundreds of years. When a sculptor went to make a statue of the god, he would take out a statue from the temple and copy it. It was supposed to be a certain canon of proportion. Or, for example, and this will surprise you, when somebody painted a tomb painting, the first thing they did was, a man would come in and put a grid on the wall like graph paper.

And next, the person who was going to draw the scene would come in—these were specialists—he would come in and he would make sure that the proportions were right by using the grid. So maybe, for example, three squares were for the head, then the shoulders had to be seven squares. Then the distance from the shoulder to the knee had to be eight squares. The proportions were always the same. They were supposed to be the same. They were basically reducing Egyptian art to paint by numbers. You were kind of filling in the boxes. And that's because there was a world order. There was a way that art was supposed to be, and it was supposed to stay that way.

So you can really trace a lot of the culture from the art, and that's why the art historians do what they do. It's very important to grasp that. I'll tell you an interesting thing—the way the Greeks viewed Egyptian art. Now, it's surprising, but Plato, the philosopher, was in some sense opposed to art. He felt that art was false, because, you know, when you do a great statue it looks like the real person. And what you're really at as a philosopher is truth; you want truth, so in a sense art was a bad thing. But if you read Plato's dialogues, he talks about Egyptian art and that was okay. Now why is Egyptian art okay to the Greeks, or to Plato a philosopher; the answer is it didn't try to fool anybody. If you look at those paintings, those strange paintings where you get a profile face but a full frontal eye, and the shoulders are squared but the head is ... it's impossible. It's not trying to fool you; it doesn't look like the person. There is a different purpose in Egyptian art. So, for the Greeks, Egyptian art was special also.

Also, reducing it to sort of paint by numbers, it was in mathematical proportions. The Greeks love numbers, and Egyptian art was almost art by the numbers. So the art historical approach is a legitimate one also, very legitimate.

But as I say, I am going to try to put some of these together, use different approaches, be broad, eclectic. And in this course you'll get a little bit of art history, you'll get a little bit of philology, but mostly we'll get events. I want to show you the events that made Egypt what it was and the people that made those events.

Let me tell you about how we know so much about ancient Egypt. As I said before, we don't know that much about the Mayans, and they're more recent. We don't know that much about the Assyrians, the Babylonians. But we know an incredible amount about the Egyptians, and let me explain that. It comes from their belief in life after death. It comes out of religion. The Egyptians were resurrectionists. That means they believe that the body, the physical body, would literally get up and go again in the next world. Now if you believe that, that the next world is in a sense a continuation of this world, you're going to kind of do the same things you did in this world in the next world. If you believe that, you put all your energies into the next world, because that's going to last a lot longer than this one. So they built tombs out of stone to last forever. And on those tomb walls they painted scenes so the gods could see how they wanted to be treated in the next world. So on the tomb walls, if a guy liked fishing, and many Egyptians loved fishing in the marshes, he would have a scene painted of himself in his boat fishing. If he liked playing games, and the Egyptians have a game similar to chess called *senet*, he would have himself painted on the wall moving the pieces. So these tomb wall scenes are a great little window into ancient Egyptian daily life. Almost everything is there. You can see guys harvesting crops. You can see women weaving. It's all there. So tombs are very important, and it's not just the paintings.

They believed you could take it with you. So they filled the tombs with everything they wanted in the next world. So when we discover an intact tomb, it's got everything. It was a little bit like, I often think of it as, imagine you're going on a trip to a country you've never been to. You're not sure what the weather is like. You're not sure what the rules are. So you take everything. You take your umbrella. You take the raincoat just in case it rains there. And that's what the Egyptians did. They tried to take everything. So when you get a complete Egyptian tomb, you get furniture. Guys took their beds, right. Women took their cosmetics. The games. If you're a pharaoh you can take your chariot. So Egyptian tombs are a wonderful source of daily life for the ancient Egyptians.

One of the reasons we know so much about Egypt is this belief in life after death. There is another great source of how we know what we know. Remember that the Egyptians had writing very early, so they left us a lot of written material, and that's important. And temple walls were like bulletin boards to the ancient Egyptians. If you wanted to tell the world something, you carved it on a temple wall, at least if you were the pharaoh.

Now what the pharaohs carved on the temple walls is a little bit surprising to our culture—battle scenes. See it kind of sounds funny to have a war scene in a temple. But remember, the Egyptians weren't into peace. They were on top of the world, and they'd like to stay there. So they wanted a constant state of war with victory after victory. So when a pharaoh came back from a victory, he would go to the temple wall and on the outside of the wall he would carve the story of his victory. And these guys were really a nation of accountants; they listed everything. So you would get the number of captives, the number of people slain. You would get even the names of the pharaoh's horses. We know the names of Ramses the Great's horses. I'll tell you that in another lecture. But they had everything there. So temple walls are a wonderful source of Egyptian history.

Also, if the pharaoh sort of wanted to get in good with the gods, he would list all the offerings he had given to the temple that year. So we will have a list of maybe 500, 600 different things that the pharaoh gave to the temple—6,000 jars of wine for the priests, 800,000 loaves of bread, 5,000 bolts of cloth, 16 vessels of sacred oils, so many rings of gold. So we have it all on temple walls. So temple walls are a wonderful source. And because of the climate in Egypt, those temple walls are still there. And you can go and see Karnak Temple, some of the walls look just like when they were built. So temple walls are a great source.

And there are more sources. We have religious texts, because they were so religious they wrote down their religion. I mean the priest— that was the job of the priests, they wrote their religion. Now one of the things about religious texts is they don't only tell you the religion, they give you an insight into fears, what the people were afraid of. For example, we have "Books of the Dead." Now a "Book of the Dead" was a guidebook of how to get to the next world. And these are long rolls of papyrus. Very often they have illustrations, paintings of the gods, and they tell you how to behave so you're going to get to the next world. They are collections of magical spells, and if you read the spells, you get an idea of what these guys were worried about. For example, there is a spell to get power in your legs. The idea was you've been mummified, you've been dead a while, now you've got to get up and go again, so you better recite the spell for power in your legs. You have to recite a spell for breath to the mouth. There is a spell for making sure that your head isn't cut off. So there were spells for all occasions. And these religious texts give us ideas of what these people were thinking; they were just like us.

Now, they didn't just put them on papyri; they carved them on their coffins. So we have what we call coffin texts, magical spells for the next world on coffins. So we have loads of religious texts, and that's another good source, and we'll talk about them also.

But there's also literature. I don't know if you realize it but the Egyptians wrote short stories, they wrote fiction, and they wrote love poetry, too. There is a wonderful genre, love poems of the 18th dynasty. It's really great stuff. So there are plenty of good sources for us to learn the history of Egypt, and we've got to use them all. So, I love to use literature. I love that, I mean, I just love reading those stories and I think you'll enjoy it, too. But there are plenty of ways we have of learning about Egypt.

Let me tell you one last source that I think is a good one; other Egyptologists think it's a bad source. It's Herodotus, a Greek tourist, and I emphasize, he was a tourist, who went to Egypt around 450 B.C. Now Herodotus was a great guy; he went everywhere. For example, he went to Russia. He went to visit the Scythians. He talks about their burials. He went down into Ethiopia; he went everywhere.

In 450 B.C. Egypt was still going on, it was a late period, and he published his work. When I say published, of course, he wrote them down. And the book that he wrote is called *Historia*. Now histories, history is the Greek word for research. All right. These were his researches. And we get our word history because this is the first history book in the world. So we call it history because Herodotus called it that. But Book Two of his research is all about Egypt. So that's a nice source, somebody who was really there, an eyewitness account in 450 B.C. of Egypt of what was going on.

Now the reason I say some people don't think he's a good source, and we have to be careful with how we use Herodotus, very careful: He didn't speak the language. He was undoubtedly working through translators, probably had a guide, like a tourist guide, and some of the things he told weren't necessarily true. He has some strange stories that he tells, really strange. For example, Herodotus says that carved on the Great Pyramid of Egypt was how many onions and bread and things the workmen were given for working on the pyramid. Now it doesn't seem right. The pharaoh is not going to build this pyramid as his tomb and then say, all right, let's put down the onions and bread the guys were given. I think what happened was that Herodotus was being taken around by this guide who was probably illiterate, couldn't read what was inscribed on the pyramid, and Herodotus says, "Hey, what does that say?" And like most guides in Egypt, he made it up. He said, "Oh, it says the bread and the beer." So there are many things that are inaccurate in Herodotus, but he's still a good source for many things. So he is one way we have of learning about ancient Egypt, and we'll be talking about Herodotus.

But let me tell you a little bit about how we're going to organize this course, how it's going to work. As I said, I'm going to try to do it by emphasizing people. Now let me say one thing about this person-centric approach, all right, sort of personalizing Egypt. There are two theories about what makes Egypt great. One of the theories is geography, that the Nile is what makes Egypt great. Now as you probably know, the Nile overflows each year, overflows it banks, and as it overflows it deposits rich topsoil that enabled the Egyptians to grow plentiful crops. And as a tremendous consequence of this, if you can grow more food than you need, you can support a large number of people, a large number of people who don't contribute to your economy. And what large number of people are you going to support? An army. Egypt could support a standing army. Now a standing army, at first, doesn't contribute to the economy, but once it marches out of Egypt, conquers foreign lands, and brings back tribute, then it's really helping the economy. So some people say that it's the Nile that made Egypt great. Even Herodotus, our tourist, he made the famous statement, he said, Egypt is the gift of the Nile. He meant that literally. That the Nile brings the soil, the very soil of Egypt, and deposits it. So that's one theory of what makes Egypt great, geography. Now I'm sure it's more than that, though, I mean, it's part of it, of course. The Nile enabled them to support also not just an army but priests. They could start having a whole leisure class that did nothing but think about religion. So the Nile is an important factor.

But also it's the personalities. Egypt was always ruled by a pharaoh, a king with absolute power, a god on earth. And if you had a pharaoh who was a great man he could do great things. So that's why I said it's also the personalities, and I'll be stressing the personalities. But as we go through this history, we're going to do it chronologically. I'm going to start at the beginning, the very beginning. And we're going to go all the way down from building the pyramids, through the great personalities, and we'll end with Cleopatra, the last ruler of

Egypt. So we will go chronologically, with some side trips. When it's appropriate, we'll do a lecture on mummification, for example, which is my specialty.

You have probably gathered by now that Egyptologists come in different flavors. There are those who are the art historians who are interested in the art. There is the philologist interested in the language. Well, my specialty is really mummification, or more broadly, diseases in the ancient world, paleopathology, old suffering. I'm interested in studying mummies to try to figure out what the Egyptians suffered from. So we'll have side tours. We'll do a separate lecture, for example, on magic. But mainly chronologically.

Now let me say something about dates. Don't try to memorize them. You won't remember them anyway, and they are not that important. I always tell my students what's important is that you get the relative chronology. In other words, it's important to know that the pyramids were built when Egypt was just beginning, that when Tutankhamen was placed in his tomb the pyramids were a thousand years old. Egypt lasted so long that they had archeologists excavating in Egypt to figure out who did what. Or when Cleopatra ruled, Tutankhamen had been dead for a thousand years. So what's important is that you get the idea of what came before what. Don't worry about the dates; they are not crucial.

Now I said the last thing I wanted to do today is tell you about the goals, what I hope that you'll get out of this course. And I have a few goals. One is I would like you all, of course, to have a broad knowledge of Egyptian history, including something about architecture, about the religion, about the politics, how it was structured. But, also, of course—and I'm not an art historian—I want you to have a better appreciation of the Egyptian art. What I would love if at the end of these lectures, you could go into a museum into the Egyptian section and look at a statute and say, "Ah, idealized form, that must be Old Kingdom." Or, "Oh, look, he looks tired, that must be the pharaoh Sesostris, or one of the Seostrises, there were several who had that look. Or, "Ah, look at that, must be Ptolemaic, must be one of the Ptolemies." So I would like you to be able to, say, take a friend on a tour of the Egyptian section, and just explain it all. And I think that's reasonable.

But maybe the most important goal is I don't want it to stop with the 48th lecture. What I would hope is that after these lectures you want to continue learning about Egypt; that's the important thing. And in the bibliography I've got societies listed that you can join, publications you can subscribe to. There is an awful lot that you can do after these lectures; and that's my real goal, that I just sort of give you the beginning of the learning.

With that said, let me tell you what we'll do next time. As I said, we're going to do it chronologically. We're going to begin at the beginning, and we will start with pre-history. Ancient Egypt before writing. So I'll see you next time.

Lecture Two
Prehistoric Egypt

Scope:

In this lesson, we will see just how old "old" is. The basic divisions of prehistory (Paleolithic, Mesolithic, Neolithic) will be discussed, and each category will be defined and its specific characteristics delineated. Here we will learn the details of how stone tools are fashioned. Once these categories are clear, we will discuss the difficulties in studying a prehistoric civilization and how its remains are dated. We discuss relative and absolute dating and the various techniques used to achieve them.

Outline

I. How old is "old"? In the seventeenth century, the Bishop of Usher's Biblical estimate set the beginning of the world at 4004 B.C. The argument against fossils and evolution—the battle against prehistoric study—was eventually challenged by both data and theory.

   A. In 1859, excavations in England revealed Stone Age tools and bones of extinct animals.

   B. In the same year, Charles Darwin published *On The Origin of Species*, a book that suggested a far more distant point of origin for mankind than the Bishop of Usher had posited.

   C. A century later, archaeologist Louis Leaky's Olduvai Gorge excavation discovered a hominid (manlike) fossil that was 1.75 million years old—and some have proposed that hominids are even older.

II. The distant human past is conventionally divided into three ages: the Paleolithic, or Old Stone Age, when humans existed as hunter-gatherers; the Mesolithic, a transition stage; and the Neolithic, or New Stone Age, when plants and animals were first domesticated. We begin with several stages of the Paleolithic.

   A. The Early Paleolithic Age dates from 700,000–70,000 B.C., when Homo Erectus lived.

1. The earliest Egyptian habitation was circa 700,000 B.C. These people perhaps migrated from the south along the Nile Valley. The climate supported fauna as found today on the Serengeti Plain—giraffes, gazelles, hippopotami.
2. The first human inhabitants used language, gathered food, used the hand axe, and perhaps controlled fire. The axe was flaked, fit nicely in the hand, and was the only tool for 70,000 years.

B. The Early Middle Paleolithic, 70,000–43,000 B.C., was the time of Neanderthal man.
1. Neanderthals were not "brute savages." They buried their dead in caves and cared for the injured and old.
2. They developed a flaking technique that provided smaller, better-formed tools, such as scrapers and daggers. Many have been found in the desert—Egypt was more moist at the time.

C. Homo Sapiens appeared during the Late Middle Paleolithic Age, from 43,000–30,000 B.C..
1. Modern man, Homo Sapiens, replaced rather than evolved from the Neanderthal.
2. One of two sources of the Nile is Lake Tana in Ethiopia. During this period, it joins the Nile for the first time, causing flooding or inundation.
3. The average life expectancy during this time was less than 30 years.

D. The Late Paleolithic Age lasted from 30,000–10,000 B.C.
1. The Nile was declining. The people lived by swamps (malaria was a problem), fished, and ate mollusks.
2. Their settlements had clay hearths on which they cooked, grindstones for grinding wild cereal grains, and pigments for eye make-up. There was no farming or cattle breeding.
3. Tools were now fashioned from quartz and diorite, as well as from flint and obsidian. The development of the sickle was an indication that plants were becoming important for food. An intensive caring for plants may indicate an early experiment in farming, but this was not yet domestication.

4. The development of the bow, the first weapon to store energy, along with the arrow, made hunting safer and easier.

5. Tools have been found in the south at Kom Ombo. They are called *microtools*—arrow points, sickle blades, and grindstones.

6. Sickles disappear for a couple of thousand years. This may indicate that early attempts at farming failed, perhaps because the climate changed or hunting became more efficient.

III. The Mesolithic Period dates from 10,000–5,000 B.C.

    A. During the Mesolithic, cosmetics for ritual use appeared.

    B. There was no pottery in the north of Egypt; ostrich eggshells were used for cooking. In the south (Sudan), pottery was developed.

    C. The human groups were very isolated, and each may have spoken its own dialect.

IV. The Neolithic Age dates from 5,000–3,200 B.C.

    A. Pottery was developed in the north.

    B. Agriculture was introduced—grains were cooked, beer was brewed.

    C. Settlements grew up along the Nile, and the first signs of kingship appeared in both the north (Lower Egypt) and the south (Upper Egypt).

    D. This was the beginning of Egyptian civilization. The population was about 2,000 people. The dead were buried, with possessions, in sand-pit burials.

    E. Carved palettes, some adorned with decorative art, were used for grinding cosmetics. This was a culture capable of more than just surviving.

V. Different kinds of dating establish the antiquity of ancient Egypt.

    A. Relative dating is not absolute and, thus, is subject to variation.

        1. Pottery is essential to dating sites. Sir Flinders Petrie's insight was that the more highly decorated pottery is newer—things evolve from the simple to the complex.

      2. Stratigraphy records layers during excavations—the higher excavations are newer.

B. Absolute dating is based on scientific examination.

      1. Carbon-14 dating is Dr. Willard Libby's discovery. All living things have the same proportion of C-14, with a half-life of 5,730 years. At death, organic material starts to decay into C-12 and nitrogen-14.

      2. Problems with this method include contamination, such as the reuse of old wood in new houses. Carbon-14 dating can be used neither for very old samples (too little C-14 remains), nor for nonliving things, such as stones and metals.

C. Paleobotany and paleozoology are, respectively, the studies of plant and animal remains. Properly studied, pollen and bones can reveal the flora and fauna of a distant period.

Essential Reading:

Michael Hoffman, *Egypt Before the Pharaohs*.

Questions to Consider:

1. What was the rate of progress like in prehistoric Egypt?

2. How do we figure out what life was like in a preliterate society?

Lecture Two—Transcript
Prehistoric Egypt

Hello again. Last time I said we were going to start chronologically, and what I would like to do today is tell you about most-ancient Egypt, prehistoric Egypt, Egypt before writing.

Now let me say something about the word "prehistoric." It's literally "before history." What that means is "before writing." So it's not a term that covers the whole world at the same time. For example, writing comes into Egypt about 3200 B.C. So after 3200 B.C. Egypt is out of prehistoric times, but England is still in prehistoric times. So it depends on the culture. It's a relative term, and prehistoric Egypt means Egypt before 3200 B.C.

Now what I'd like to do today is tell you about how old "old" is, just how far back these prehistoric times go. And I would also like to tell you how prehistorians divide up this period. They divide it into three chunks called Paleolithic, Mesolithic, and Neolithic, and I'll be talking about those. And I am also going to say something about stone tools, how they're made and why they're important. At the end, I'd like you to know how we know all this stuff, how did prehistorians figure this out if they don't have any written documents.

So let's start with how old is old. Now the study of prehistory is fairly recent. Before we really got into scientific prehistory, there was just the Bible. And people were using the Bible to try to figure out how far back time went. In the 17ᵗʰ century, the Bishop of Usher, using the Bible figuring out from generations, the begets—so and so begets so and so, begets so and so—and working backwards figured out that the world began in 4004 B.C. That was his calculation. And you could actually buy in the 17ᵗʰ century the authorized Bible, which had in the margin, right by Genesis, when it's talking about everything beginning, in the margin it says, 4004 B.C. So that was when the world began.

Now a later colleague of the Bishop of Usher went further and he did some fine-tuning of the calculation. Agreeing with 4004 B.C., he said it was October 23ʳᵈ and about 9 in the morning; that's when the Lord decided to do it all. So that's how far prehistory went back in the 17ᵗʰ century. And, you know, the Bishop of Usher wasn't the only one who believed that. Isaac Newton, the great physicist, great mathematician, inventor of calculus—Isaac Newton in his spare time tried to work out the chronology of ancient Egypt. He wrote a book on the chronology of ancient Egypt. Remember the first lecture where I was talking about how Egypt is a wonderful escapism? That's what Newton was using it as; when he got tired of calculations he would figure out Egyptian chronology. And in his book, Newton says, the Egyptians were really brash, they traced their history back far too far, past 4004 B.C. So Newton also agreed that prehistory didn't go back all that far.

Now the real scientific study of prehistory begins in the year 1859. Two things happen, and it's an interesting story. The first is that a few antiquarians, men interested in the Old World, started excavating in England, and what they found were stone tools, Stone Age tools, and next to the Stone Age tools were the bones of extinct animals. And they started publishing their findings, and they realized that extinct animals probably went back further than 4004 B.C. So they were suggesting, because of the combination of the stone tools and extinct animals, that history maybe went back further than the Bishop of Usher thought. That's the first event that happened in 1859.

The second event was the publication of one of the most important books in the history of the world, Darwin's *Origin of Species*. Darwin suggested that we are the products of evolution, and that took a long time, evolution. It didn't happen in just a couple of thousand years. So between Darwin's evolution of the origin of species, and finding stone implements with fossils, people were starting to think the world was a lot older than the Bishop of Usher suggested. Now also, think about the factors in evolution, what Darwin was talking about, what makes us special. For example, our eyes are placed in such a way that they are on the same plain. We're not like fish, and we have stereoscopic vision. We can see things in depth. What that means is our sight becomes more important than our sense of smell. Other factors that take place throughout evolution—our opposable thumb. We have fine motor skills. We can move our fingers for little fine-tuning of things. We can make tools; we can build things. So the opposable thumb is also an important thing that Darwin talks about.

Our teeth evolved. We don't have teeth just like apes. We have molars, for example, good for grinding grains, rather than canine teeth for ripping. So all of these evolutionary things took a long time. History had to go back much farther. Now, how much further? Well, first, in geological times, the current estimate for the origin of the world (earth) is four and a half billion years. So the Bishop was off by a few.

But what about man; how far do we go back? Well, the answer is in terms of four and a half billion years, we go back just a few moments. One of the early, early, early findings of early, early man is Louis B. Leakey's work, Louis Leakey at Olduvai Gorge in Africa. His work suggests—he found fossils of what we call hominoids. Hominoids are humanlike man. They are fossils but they are not quite—-they look like men but they are not quite us yet. His work suggests about 1.75 million years. That's how far back he pushed it, and some people are pushing it back even a little further. The envelope right now seems about two million years, maybe, that hominoids appear. All right, so it's back a long ways.

Now this is a very long, very, very long period of time to deal with, 1.75 million years. How do you cover the history of that? Well, prehistorians divide up prehistory into three big manageable junks. There are the Paleolithic, Mesolithic, and Neolithic—three big chunks. And we're going to talk about each of those.

But let me give you a little bit of definition. Paleolithic, again, most of it comes from the Greek: *paleo*, of course, is "old," *lithos* is "stone." So that's the Old Stone Age. Now what characterizes the Old Stone Age is that man during this period is a hunter and gatherer. There are no domesticated animals. There is no raising of crops. He's hunting and gathering. That is the characteristic of Paleolithic.

Now let me jump to Neolithic. Neolithic is when finally we get domestication of animals and the raising of crops—the New Stone Age. Then the Mesolithic is what's left, and it's, of course, *meso*, in the middle, it's the Middle Stone Age and that's the transition period. That's when we go from hunter-gatherer, and there is a sliding in, and it's a gradual sliding in, that's when we go to raising crops and animals.

Now let say something about when Egypt is first populated, though, Louis B. Leakey's 1.75 million is further south. Egypt is first populated about 700,000 B.C. 700,000 B.C. The general feeling, and this is far from established, is that these early inhabitants of the Nile Valley came in through the south, from Africa, of course, but through the south. Now this was an easy transition for them, these people coming in, coming north. Egypt was not always desert. People tend to think of Egypt as desert. But in 700,000 B.C. it was like the Serengeti Plain. You had giraffes, gazelles. It was lush, and the Nile was the kind of corridor you could follow. You had a water supply. So these people came in from the south to the north. Let me emphasize, we don't have their remains. There are no bones of these people, but we have their tools, and we'll talk about that.

Now what were these people like? Well, they had speech. They could probably control fire. These were not super-crude people. And they were food gatherers. And they had one tool and only one tool— the hand ax. Now the hand ax is a tool that is as simple as you can imagine. It's a stone that you hold in your hand and you use it to smash something that's softer than it. It's not an accidental tool, though; it's not something you just pick up on the ground and use. The thing about a hand ax is it's flaked. It's made to fit the palm of your hand; that's the idea of it. It will fit nicely, won't cut into your hand, and you can use it for smashing things. It's an intentional tool. We can tell by looking at a tool if it's been flaked, and these are clearly flaked. So we have one tool—the hand ax.

One of the things I'm going to stress today is how the rate of progress has changed in the world today. From 700,000 B.C. to roughly 70,000 B.C., the only tool is the hand ax. There is no other tool than the hand ax. Now think about how things have changed in the last 200 years, how much change we've had. Then think about how much change we've had in the last 100 years. How about the last 20 years, the computer revolution. So things are changing at a tremendous rate, increasingly changing, change is increasing, the rate of change is increasing. But for nearly half a million years, we've got no progress, just the hand ax. Remarkable thing.

Now the next big jump is around 70,000 B.C. Around 70,000 B.C., we get Neanderthal man coming into the Nile Valley. Now the word Neanderthal is German, because most of the early prehistoric studies were done in Europe, and the fossils of this man were found in the Neander Valley, and German for valley is "*thal.*" So Neanderthal man is the man found in Neander Valley.

Now people always use the phrase Neanderthal as if he was a caveman, a brute. These people were not brutes; they were not. They buried their dead. They cared for the sick. And they developed a little more sophisticated flaking technique for tools. For example, they now have specialized tools. They have scrapers, which are intended for scraping hides. You can take a scraper, which is only maybe four inches long, hold it in your hand, remove the flesh very easily, then remove the hair from the hide, and you've got the beginnings of a garment for clothing. So they've got these specialized tools. Neanderthal man is not this brute creature that people think. I mean, for example, if you dressed him up and put him on the subway you wouldn't notice him, he'd fit right in, he's not what people think. So these are people who are eking out a survival in the Nile Valley some time after 70,000 B.C. to around 43,000 B.C.

And let me say something about where we find these tools. Neanderthal tools—the scrapers, the hand axes—are found in the desert, very often in the desert. What that means is that Egypt was much more moist; it wasn't desert when they were making the tools there. They weren't going out into the middle of the desert. So in Egypt, the climate has changed considerably and that's important.

Now, our next big shift is around 43,000 B.C. We get modern man, us, homo sapiens. Let me emphasize that we didn't evolve out of Neanderthal man; homo sapiens replaces him. There is not enough time for evolution here. But let me say some things about what we did when we did come into the Nile Valley. We fished. The Nile starts to dry up a little bit at this time, and there are little gatherings of people around lakes. They ate mollusks, shellfish. And if you ask me what kind of communities were there, the best estimate from tools found is there were bands or clans of maybe 25 to 50 people living together at a time. What's our life expectancy? Less than 30. From birth, you could not expect to live more than 30 years. That was life in prehistoric times.

Now there are also new tools coming in. We're going to fashion tools out of different materials. The first, of course, was flint; it's the easiest to flake. But there was also obsidian, which is volcanic glass. Now the advantage of obsidian is it gives you a much sharper edge. It's as a sharp as surgical steel. So they are fashioning tools out of other materials—diorite, a harder stone; quartzite is used. And during this period we're going to get a new tool: the sickle. Now let me emphasize the sickle is used for harvesting crops, but that does not mean that they were planting crops.

First, how did you make a sickle in prehistoric times? Well, you took the wood—the crescent part—and you inserted into it flints, about two, three inches long, and you had a whole row of these, and that's how you could harvest your grain. But the general theory during this time is that they weren't planting grain, they were sort of intensively caring for wild grains. They hadn't yet gotten the click that you can actually plant your own.

They're also introducing the bow and arrow during this period. Now that's an important invention. The bow is the first weapon in history that stores energy. By bending the wood and storing it in a string, it can all be transferred to the arrow when it's shot. This, of course, means that you have to have arrowheads, and indeed they flake arrow points. Now this is not easy. It is not easy at all to flake something like this with a crescent so you can attach it to the shaft, but they do it, and they have even more impressive tools.

At Kom Ombo, which is a site in Egypt in the south, they have found arrow points that we call microtools. They are tiny; they are the size of your thumbnail. An arrow point the size of your thumbnail, which is used for hunting birds. Now imagine the skill required to flake something like that. So they are really developing their tool making. See, progress is coming faster. First we had half a million years with only the hand ax; now we've got the bow, the sickle, arrows—things are starting to happen.

Now one strange thing happens with the sickle, and this is an archeological puzzle that is not fully settled yet. The sickle disappears for a couple of thousand years. The sickle appears, they seem to be harvesting crops, and then it disappears for a few thousand years. What happened? Well, the dominant theory is crop failure, that for some reason the crops failed, and they are no longer harvesting, so you don't need the sickle. It will be introduced again, but later.

I'll tell you another theory, just a possibility. It's a long shot, I'd say, but it's a possibility. With the bow and arrow, hunting becomes a lot easier. You can be removed from the animal at a safe distance and shoot your arrow and it may mean that protein gathering through hunting becomes a more important source of food than even the gathering of the crops. It could be. So perhaps the bow being introduced, perhaps it's crop failure, but things are starting to happen.

Now we're entering the Mesolithic period. This is around 10,000 B.C. This is going to be the transition from hunter-gatherers into domestication of animals, raising of crops. This is the period, the Mesolithic, when people start to settle. They have grindstones upon which they can grind whatever grain they get, but they also grind cosmetics, eye makeup. This is an important part of the culture. It's probably both religious, ritual, and maybe also just pure decorative. So they take green, which is malachite, and put it on their eyes, mix it with a little bit of fat that binds it, and you start to get cosmetics.

And then we start to get real civilization as we know it. We're going to enter the Neolithic period, the New Stone Age. This is when we get pottery. Now something about pottery that is surprising: Pottery is not as easy to develop as you may think. We take it for granted, but think of what it involves. Finding the right clay, and you have to build a kiln to fire it, you have to fire it some way, and that's not such an easy thing to do. It's a big step, but pottery does wonderful things for you. You can now cook the grains that you've harvested. You can make a kind of porridge. You can also make beer, which makes life better. Interestingly, by the way, in archeological excavations, whenever you find a bakery, right next to it is the brewery, because they both use yeast. So almost always in ancient Egypt you find a bakery, you look for the brewery. You find a brewery, you look for the bakery. So they are able to cook their food in pots now. We're starting to get real settlements.

Now, what do I mean by a real settlement? In the beginning it's probably villages of about 150 people, up and down the Nile. But with toolmaking, making little arrowheads, you need skilled labor. So now we get division of labor. We get the toolmaker, we get a baker, we get a brewer, we get the pot maker. We're starting to get organized society up and down the Nile. This is the Neolithic period. This is leading up to the written word in Egypt.

Now, also we start to get politics. In this early period, at the end of prehistory but before writing, before 3200 B.C., we start to get all these villages up and down the Nile, and, by the way, the population of Egypt I think will surprise you at this period. It's about 2,000; that's the entire population of Egypt, these isolated villages. But toward the end of this period, they seem to have kings, Upper and Lower Egypt, two divisions of Egypt. Each one seems to be ruled by a single ruler. So we're getting a kind of low-level unification, a social strata, a political strata; each is ruled by a king. Now one of the things you have to remember about Egypt is Upper Egypt is on the bottom and Lower Egypt is on the top, because the Nile flows from the south to the north. So we refer to "up the Nile" as going south and "down the Nile" as going north. That's why Upper Egypt is below Lower Egypt, so remember that.

But we're starting to get civilization as we know it. Now these people, these Neolithic people, New Stone Age people, they have all kinds of things. They start burying their dead in sandpit burials, and these sandpit burials are perhaps the origin of mummification. If you bury a body in the sand, it dehydrates naturally. It's a natural mummy that we get when we find these early burials. But more important about these burials, is the people are buried with possessions. They are not just chucked in a pit to get rid of them. When you bury someone with pots, with jewelry, the suggestion is a belief in life after death. So even before writing, we can try to make some inferences about what these people thought. And burials is just one aspect.

They also carved their slate palettes. Now a palette has a flat surface, for grinding the cosmetics I was talking about. But they carved them in the shapes of animals—sometimes whimsical animals—a hippopotamus, a turtle. And they would grind their cosmetics. This is a sign that life is perhaps getting a little easier. You can kind of lay back and do a little bit of art. These are people who care about the finer things in life.

They also had little statutes, little figurines made out of clay, of women, often these wide-hipped women. Very often it is suggested that these figurines are fertility symbols. They could well be, but we have to be careful, we don't know for sure; they could just be figurines.

They also have decorated pots, and that's going to be important. They have black-top pots. Now what's black top—it's a red, Nile clay pot, but it has a very nice black rim. And the way they did that was, you take your pot and you invert it in a fire and it carbonizes the rim. So they have decorations. They have incisions on the pots. Maybe little wavy lines to indicate that it's a water pot. Later, they'll even paint the pots with ostriches and boats and palm trees. There is an art production here. These aren't just people who are struggling to survive; they've got more than just that.

Now, let me say something about the pottery, because pottery is absolutely crucial. In any excavation, you pray that you find pottery. Why? Pottery is virtually indestructible. Granted, pots break, but the fragments remain forever in any kind of soil. And this is one way we date a site. This is how we know what we know about Egypt. And it's really the result of one man, Flinders Petrie. Now Sir Flinders Petrie, he was a great guy, really a wild man. He used to walk 20 miles a day. He would walk, and on Fridays he would walk 20 miles one way, get the payment for his men, come back, and pay them. Remarkable man. He wasn't trained as an Egyptologist; there were no Egyptologists in the 19th century when Petrie started. He was a surveyor, went out to survey the pyramids, fell in love with Egypt, and excavated for the next 70 years. And Petrie made the interesting observation, he said, you can tell which site is earlier than another by the pottery. Now in his day, everybody was looking for treasure. They were looking for gold; they were looking for statues. Petrie was looking for knowledge. And he excavated in places that nobody else wanted to excavate. He would look at places that weren't promising, but they had pottery. And he would go there and he'd say, think of it this way: Let's say you find one site with a pot, typical water pot that's undecorated. Good. Now another village has pots, perhaps—or another site has pots—with wavy lines and size. Same kind of pot, same shape, but wavy lines, maybe indicating it's water. Great. Now you find another site that has the same kind of pot, wavy lines, and handles. This is fancier. This is the late model. And what Petrie realized was things go from the simple to the complex. So we can use pottery to date a site by whether it's complex, whether it's simple, and this was all due to Sir Flinders Petrie.

So pottery is crucial to prehistorians, where there is no written record. That's how we date; that's called relative dating. You don't know exactly how old it is, but you know it's earlier than the other site.

Another way of getting a relative date is what we call stratigraphy, layers. If you excavate a site, usually people don't move. People in a village, they die, the next generation, they build, and the site builds up, it gets higher and higher as people build newer houses on top of the older. And this is what we call a tell, a mound. And when you go to a village and you see a tell, you know, of course, that the oldest sites, the earliest occupation is on the bottom of the tell. So when you excavate you're very careful to record the level you find something at, because then you know this is earlier, this is even earlier, this is still earlier. So stratigraphy is an important part of archaeology for the prehistorian. But it doesn't give you an absolute date; it won't tell you 6,000 B.C.

That's where carbon-14 dating comes in, a relatively new development. Now, carbon-14 dating is based on a principle that everything that's alive, everything that's alive, has carbon in it. And carbon-14 is unstable. It breaks down when we start dying. Every living thing has the same proportion of carbon-14—plants, animals, we do. But when we die, it starts decaying, breaking down. Now carbon-14 has a half-life of 5,730 years. What that means is, if you have one gram of carbon-14, if you're patient, if you wait 5,730 years, you'll have half a gram. Wait another 5,730, you'll have a quarter of a gram. So if we find some material in a dig that was once alive, maybe a tree used as a beam in a house, we can carbon-14 date it and get a rough approximation of when that thing died, when it stopped. So carbon-14 dating is crucial in giving us a date for a prehistoric site. Crucial.

But there are limitations. It won't work for supernal things. It won't work for a million years old. And it won't work for things that weren't alive. You can't carbon-14 date a stone; it never took in carbon. So there are limitations, and we have to be careful, for example, that we don't use something that's been reused. Somebody might take a beam, a piece of wood and put it in a house and reuse it and the beam is 1,000 years older than the house. So you have to be very careful.

Let me tell you about one other important technique in prehistory—looking at ancient plants. We use on excavation sites paleobotanists. These are people who can look at the pollen and tell you what plants were alive at the time of the excavation. You might even be able to figure out what season, by what was in flower, when the house collapsed. And we also use paleozoologists. These are the guys who can tell you from an animal bone, "Oh, they were—that's pig, they were definitely domesticating pigs." And if you look at the bone carefully, you can even see butcher marks sometimes, so you know,

"Ah, that was slaughtered," it wasn't, just didn't die. So very often the prehistorian uses a whole bunch of people—the pot man, the paleobotanist, the paleozoologist, all of these are needed to reconstruct the very earliest part of Egyptian history.

But next time—let me tell you what we'll do next time—next time I want to also cover an area that is also in a sense prehistoric. I want to talk about ancient Egyptian mythology, the time before time began.

Lecture Three
Ancient Egyptian Thought

Scope:

In this lecture, we will try to understand how the ancient Egyptians thought. We will use three concepts to delineate different kinds of thinking: mythology, religion, and philosophy. By the end of this lecture, the student should understand the differences among these concepts and see how they played a role in the life of the ancient Egyptians.

Outline

I.   Mythology, religion, and philosophy try to answer nonempirical questions—the "big" ones that science can't answer.

  A. Is there life after death?

  B. How did the universe begin (before the Big Bang)?

  C. Is there a God?

II. Mythology contains stories that are not to be taken literally but answer basic questions about the nature of the universe. Myths have a message, then, but can't be taken literally. Unlike religion, mythology takes place in primordial time, outside of chronology or calendar time.

  A. The basic Egyptian myth described the primordial eight gods—the Ogdoad—in the primordial waters. These gods came in pairs.

  1. Hok and Hoket represent formlessness.

  2. Kuk and Kuket are darkness.

  3. Amun and Amunet are hiddenness.

  4. Nun and Nunet are the primordial waters.

  5. Together, the eight gods represent Chaos and are often depicted with the heads of frogs.

  6. The primordial hill rises out of these waters.

  7. Atum, a god, stood on that hill. He created himself, then generated the other gods.

B. The Ennead added an additional nine elemental Egyptian gods. This is quite different from Genesis and the four basic elements of the Greeks.

    1. Atum's children were Shu (air) and Tefnut (moisture).

    2. Shu and Tefnut begat Geb (earth) and Nut (sky).

    3. Geb and Nut give birth to two pairs, each of them sister and brother and wife and husband: Isis and Osiris and Seth and Nephthys. Although Seth is evil, the three others are elementally good.

C. Isis and Osiris were central to the Egyptian belief in life after death.

    1. Isis and Osiris descend to earth to civilize Egypt. While Osiris goes to teach the rest of the world how to be civilized, Isis keeps her evil brother Seth in check.

    2. Seth tricks Osiris into climbing into what will become his coffin, nails the coffin shut, then throws it in the Nile. After Osiris dies, Isis journeys to Byblos to recover her husband's body and returns to Egypt to bury it properly.

    3. Seth finds the body of Osiris and hacks it into thirteen pieces, scattering them over the Nile. Isis and Nephthys find all the pieces except the phallus and reassemble Osiris. Isis breathes life into her husband, and he is resurrected—the first person to resurrect, the first "mummy."

    4. Osiris becomes the God of the Dead; his story is the original lesson in the importance of staying at home and remaining whole. Henceforth, it will be important to be buried on Egyptian soil and to be buried complete, both prerequisites for resurrection.

    5. Isis gives birth to Horus, who defeats his Uncle Seth in battle. Horus loses his eye in the struggle, which is magically regenerated.

    6. Seth, however, doesn't die: evil will always be with us.

III. In religion, by contrast, the concept of belief is essential. Religion includes stories believed to be historical, such as the account of Moses in the Bible, that take place in chronological time.

IV. Philosophy deals with the same questions as religion does.

    A. Unlike religion, however, philosophy requires a proof based on logic.

    B. The answers to the great philosophical questions are not matters of opinion but facts that are unknown. It's not that the great questions are relative, but that we don't, given our limited perspective, have answers to them.

    C. Did the universe have no beginning, or did it begin from nothing?

        1. Such philosophical questions are important, but whether the Egyptians "did" philosophy per se is not revealed to us in their documents.

        2. Could such an advanced civilization have been ignorant of philosophy? Perhaps they simply refused to commit it to papyrus.

Essential Reading:

Erik Hornung, *Conceptions of God in Ancient Egypt.*

Supplementary Reading:

Sigfried Morenz, *Egyptian Religion.*

Questions to Consider:

1. How do religion, mythology, and philosophy differ?
2. Did the Egyptians "do" philosophy?

Lecture Three—Transcript
Ancient Egyptian Thought

Hello again. I'm glad you're back. Last time I tried to cover 700,000 years of history in half an hour. Understand it's totally inadequate; prehistorians do courses that cover an entire year on the prehistory of Egypt. So I tried to do the best we could in 30 minutes, but you should go on and read more about the area. It's important.

Now, let me say what we'll do today and then I'll try to do it. What I'd like to do is cover ancient Egyptian thought, specifically mythology, but I'm going to cover more. I'm going to cover mythology, religion, and philosophy—three different kinds of things, three different kinds of thinking. And my hope is that at the end of the lecture you'll know the difference between the three and you will be able to see what part they played in the ancient Egyptian world.

Now let me say something about what's in common for the three. Mythology, religion, and philosophy all try to answer the same kinds of questions. They answer non-empirical questions, questions that you can't answer by looking, seeing, observing. For example, is there life after death? Everybody wonders about that. And philosophy tries to answer it, religion tries to answer it, and mythology tries to answer it, but in different ways, and we'll see those ways. Another question—a typical non-empirical, philosophical, religious, mythological question—how did the universe begin? Everybody wonders. These three disciplines try to answer those also. So there are lots of questions—I mean, existence of God, the big one. All three cover it, but they do it in three very different ways, and that's what I'm going to try to show today, the differences.

Now, let's start with mythology, because this is the one that the ancient Egyptians certainly did the most of. Now, first, let me say something: Mythology tries to answer questions like, is there a God? Is there life after death? How did the universe begin? But it's not to be taken literally. Mythology gives you stories. You're supposed to listen to them very carefully. Don't take them literally, but you're supposed to get the message; that's the crucial thing. There is a message that you're supposed to get. If you listen carefully to the myth, you will learn about the beginning of the universe, how it began. If you listen carefully, you will learn about whether there is a

God or not. You will find out if there is life after death, but you can't take it literally, the story. So there is a message, but it's not literal. It's different from a fairy tale, for example; that's just a story you listen to and doesn't necessarily have a punch line. Myths always have a punch line.

Now, also, when do myths take place? They take place in what's called primordial time, time before time began. Now, it sounds like a contradiction, of course, but what we mean is, don't ask historical questions of mythological characters. For example, remember when we talked about the Bishop of Usher trying to figure out exactly when the universe began by using the Bible. Well, the Bible is a religion; that's not a myth. So the Bishop believed that it made sense to try to calculate on what day the world began, because the Bible is intended to be taken as history. Moses was a real character, historical. But with mythology we don't ask such questions. It doesn't make sense to ask, what was Zeus's birthday? It's an inappropriate question. So mythology takes place in what we call primordial time; that's different from chronological time, calendar time, our kind of time.

Now let me say the kinds of questions that we'll deal with. The Egyptians had many myths, and they had different myths for different occasions. I'm going to try to show you how the Egyptians presented the beginning of the universe and the question of life after death, how they answered that. So let's start in the very beginning.

Now for the Egyptians, in the beginning was water. And in the primordial waters were eight gods. Now, the eight gods are called the Ogdoad, O-G-D-O-A-D, it's just eight. These gods came in pairs, so to speak, a husband and wife or a male and a female. And they had attributes. So in these primordial waters were these eight gods, four pairs. You had Hok and Hoket. Now their attribute was formlessness, formlessness. Now, if you want to remember which is the male and which is the female of the pair, the female always ended in "T," the letter "T." So Hok is the male, Hoket is the female. Nice thing, by the way, about the Egyptian language—every Egyptian word that's feminine ends in a "T." Unlike say French when you're always trying to figure out why is this masculine and why is this—you don't have to worry about it in Egypt—everything ends in a "T" if it's feminine. So Hok and Hoket are the first pair; they're formlessness.

Then comes Kuk and Kuket, darkness. Amun and Amunet are next, hiddenness. Now, Amun is later going to become a very important god in ancient Egypt, the most important. But that's thousands of years off. That's when we're going to have the pharaoh Amunhotep, whose name means Amun is pleased. So we've got three pairs so far. The last, the fourth pair, is Nun and Nunet. Nun is the primordial waters, the waters themselves, and his consort, Nunet.

Now, the important thing about this myth is to gather what, just what are the Egyptians trying to tell us. Eight gods in the water? No, they are telling us more. Think about the attributes: formlessness, darkness, hiddenness … in the beginning was chaos. These are not sort of user-friendly terms—hiddenness, darkness, formlessness—they are not positive attributes; they are negative. So in the beginning we have chaos, and that's the eight, that's the beginning of the universe.

But we don't have people yet, and we don't have gods in the Egyptian sense of gods that can direct with people. These eight gods are often shown as having the heads of frogs, because they are water deities. But we don't know anymore about them really except their attributes. But then the moment of creation takes place. Out of the waters arises the primordial hill, a mound of earth. Now up and down Egypt they built temples, and every temple claimed, "We're built on the primordial hill." So, they wanted a kind of primacy. But the myth says there was a primordial hill, and standing on that primordial hill was a god Atum. Now Atum is a special god. He begins the other gods; he creates the gods that interact with earth. He is called the self-created, right. I mean, how did Atum get there? Created himself.

And then Atum by himself has two children. Now, what's going to happen is Atum is going to have, well, a total of eight gods. Atum plus the eight are called the Nine, the Ennead, nine just means ennead. So Atum starts it all off and who are his children? Shu and Tefnut. Shu is air, and as you know he's the male, right, because Tefnut ends in a "T." So Shu is air. Tefnut is moisture. So what the myth is telling us is that in the beginning we have air and moisture.

Now it's kind of interesting to compare myths; I like to compare them. Think about the first line of Genesis. I'll just read it. "In the beginning God created the heavens and the earth. Now the earth was a formless void. There was darkness over the deep." Notice there is a similarity, that in the beginning there is a formless void, darkness. Now, of course, the Egyptian myth was thousands of years earlier than the Old Testament, and we'll see possible borrowing from Egyptian mythology for Christianity and Judaism. But, the point is, people seem to agree the beginning was a scary time.

So now we have Shu and Tefnut, air and moisture. Next they have two children, Geb and Nut; again, you know who the female is, Nut. Geb is earth. Nut is the sky goddess. Nut is sometimes shown in tombs, and there is a wonderful painting of her sometimes in royal tombs. She's shown on the ceiling of a tomb, and what she is doing is bending over with her arms kind of down one wall and her legs down another, her belly is the ceiling, and it shows the stars on her belly. And what Nut does is she swallows the sun in the evening, it travels through her, and she gives birth to it in the morning. So you get this notion of birth and rebirth. So we have now, air and moisture, and we have earth and sky.

Compare that with the Greeks, by the way. Remember the Greeks had four basic elements. They had fire, air, water, and earth, and there are similarities. Interestingly, by the way, for the Greeks, fire was a very special element. It's the only of the four elements that animals don't live in. Animals lived in the earth, and the air, and the water, but not in fire. And fire in later ages will become a crucial element. But we have the Egyptian myth.

Now, we've got Geb and Nut, sky and earth. There is even a sidebar to this myth where you've got a story of how air becomes a little jealous of Geb and Nut and squeezes in between the air and the heavens and the earth. Anyway, they give birth to four gods who are central to Egyptian mythology. They give birth to Isis and Osiris, who are brother and sister, naturally, and husband and wife. By the way, I said that every Egyptian name that's feminine ends in a "T," but I said Isis. It doesn't end in a "T." That's because we know her name from the Greeks. Her real name in Egyptian is Ist, I-S-T, but the Greeks when they came and added their "is" endings, Ist becomes Isis. All right, so sometimes it won't sound right, but it does in ancient Egyptian. Isis and Osiris are brother and sister, husband and wife. This, by the way, will justify what pharaohs do later in marrying their own sisters. So we're going to get a lot from this myth.

Now they have a brother and sister also; there are four children involved here. They are Seth and Nebthet. Now Seth is sometimes Set, sometimes Seth, same god; he's the male. And Nebthet, Greek version Nephthys, are also brother and sister, husband and wife. These four—Isis, Osiris, Seth, and Nebthet—are going to be crucial. And I want to explain to you today the myth of Isis and Osiris. According to the myth—now remember in a myth you're supposed to listen carefully and you'll get the message—you will see at the end of this myth you will get almost all of the basics of the Egyptian belief in life after death.

Isis and Osiris are the good guys. They are elementally good gods, want to do well. Nebthet also, their sister, is a good goddess, but Seth is elementally evil. He's the archetype of the devil, only tries to do harm. Now, according to the myth, Isis and Osiris come down to earth to civilize Egypt. Now, remember when we talked about prehistory; what does civilization mean? It means domesticating animals. It means raising crops. So we learn that the origins of civilization, domestication of crops and animals comes from Egypt, Egypt is the source, at least that's what the Egyptians said.

Now Isis and Osiris do such a good job of civilizing Egypt, bringing civilization to the people of the Nile Valley, that Osiris goes away to teach the rest of the world how to do these things. So we get the diffusion of civilization from Egypt to other lands. Now, while Osiris is away, Seth tries to do horrible things to Egypt, but fortunately Isis is very powerful. She is the goddess of magic. She is even called "she who knows all the names." Now what that means is, if you wanted to do a magic spell against somebody, I would have to know your name so I could say, "May this happen to Megan," for example, "May this happen to Marvin." Now, Isis knows everybody's name. When an Egyptian kid was born, they often had two names. One was the real name and only his mother knew that name; the other name was the name that everybody knew. So, for example, if we name you Marvin but we really call you Harry, everybody knows you by Harry and if somebody tries to do an evil spell on you and says, "Oh, may Harry break his leg," it won't work, because your name is really Marvin. So Isis, as having the name "she who knows everyone's name," means nobody is out of her range. She is the super hero.

So Isis, who is powerful, keeps her evil brother Seth in check; nothing terrible happens to Egypt. And then Osiris returns, having civilized other countries. Now, Seth, though, is always scheming and he lays a plan. While Osiris is sleeping, while his brother is sleeping, he takes his exact measurements, his bodily measurements, and he builds a wooden chest to those exact proportions, exactly to the proportions of Osiris. And at a banquet he says, "I'll give a wonderful prize to anybody who fits exactly into this chest." And guest after guest tries, doesn't quite fit, a little too big, a little too small. It was very much like Cinderella's slipper. And finally Osiris tries, and it fits him just right, of course. But Seth is ready and he nails the chest shut, pours molten lead on the chest, and throws it into the Nile. And Osiris dies in the chest.

Now, interesting, by the way, there is no contradiction involved in someone being a god and dying. He is a god greater than man but mortal. So in the chest Osiris dies. But the myth doesn't end there. The Nile flows northward to the Mediterranean, and the chest washes ashore at Byblos, modern Lebanon. And, according to the myth, there is this huge storm and the chest is blown into the branches of a tree with dead Osiris. Now the tree grows to tremendous proportions, encompassing the chest in the trunk. The king of Byblos wants to build a palace, and he needs large trees, cedars of Lebanon, he needs large trees for pillars, and this tree is cut down and incorporated into the palace. It becomes a pillar. So we get the strange situation of Osiris in a chest in a pillar in a palace, but that's the way it is.

But Isis, the devoted wife, sets out on a journey to recover the body of her husband. She eventually finds out where Osiris is in this pillar in a palace, talks to the queen of Byblos, gets a job as her handmaiden, talks, and explains, "My husband is in this pillar in the palace." The queen is sympathetic; the pillar is cut down. The chest is taken out and Osiris is indeed there dead. Isis brings the body back to Egypt for proper burial.

Seth, always scheming, finds the body. He finds the properly buried body of Osiris and hacks it into thirteen pieces, scatters them up and down the Nile. There are different places where different pieces are buried. Isis, wanting to give her husband the proper burial, finds the pieces. She is aided by her sister Nebthet, who wants to help. They find almost all of the pieces of Osiris; the phallus is missing. It was thrown into the Nile and devoured by fish.

Actually, it's interesting that even in the myth, the name of the fish, the name of the three fish that devour the phallus, is given. It's quite interesting because the fish are electric, mildly electric, so I think they were special. So, anyway, the phallus is devoured, but Isis finds the other twelve pieces, reassembles Osiris, fashions an artificial phallus for Osiris so he's complete, says magical words, and breathes life into Osiris. She takes the form of a bird. There are many scenes of her taking the form of a bird, hovering over her husband. And Osiris resurrects. He becomes the first person ever to resurrect. And as a resurrected one, he becomes the God of the Dead. So Osiris is the God of Dead. In a sense, he is the first mummy.

Now, what are we supposed to learn from this myth? I mean, we're supposed to listen carefully and get the message. Well, as I said, almost every funerary belief that the Egyptians had can be traced from this. For example, it is crucial for Isis to recover the body and bury it on Egyptian soil; that's why she goes to Byblos. There is something special about Egypt and Egyptian soil. This, by the way, is why the Egyptians never colonized. They never, when they conquered a foreign country, set up a big colony. Nobody wanted to die away from Egypt. You had to be brought back to Egypt, mummified, buried in the soil. So the first thing is, you have to be buried in Egyptian soil.

Next, Osiris was missing one part, the phallus. Isis creates an artificial phallus. You must be complete. Because if you're going to resurrect, if you're going to use this body again in the next world, you want it to be complete. So you have to have a complete body. This, by the way, was a practice that was followed by Egyptian embalmers. When a person died who had only one leg, had a leg amputated, they would create an artificial leg, an early prosthetic device, but for the next world. So we're also learning that you have to be complete.

Now think about the chest that Seth fashions, it's to the exact proportions of Osiris. This is going to become later the anthropoid coffin, those coffins that we're so familiar with in Egyptian art that are shaped like a man. That chest in the Osiris myth becomes the anthropoid coffin. So we have also the belief that there is going to be a special container for the body that is going to preserve it. And if you have that special container, that coffin, if you are complete, if your body is whole, if you're buried on Egyptian soil, then like Osiris, you too can resurrect and go to the next world. So it's a very, very important myth.

And it doesn't even end there. Isis and Osiris have a child, Horus, who does battle with his evil uncle, Seth, who has killed his father. And one of the important things that we get out of this battle is he defeats Seth, he beats him in battle, but two things happen. One is Horus's eye is taken out in the battle, but it's magically regenerated, so good triumphs. But the other important thing from that battle is that Horus defeats Seth, but he doesn't kill him. And I think it's a little bit like, and there is a message there, it's a little like *Star Wars* where until the very end, you remember, Darth Vader always gets away. I think it's an existential statement: Evil will always be with us; we have to be vigilant. That's why Seth isn't killed in the myth. There is a real basic truth that they're telling you.

But this is a crucial thing to the Egyptians—mythology. I don't think they meant it literally; I don't think they meant you're supposed to really believe this actually happened, but you're getting certain basic truths. Every deceased person after he was dead was called by his own name and Osiris. So, for example, your name might be Annie Osiris, Nachman Osiris. The idea was you wanted to be associated with Osiris. Osiris resurrected and if we call you Osiris, you too will resurrect. So the myth tells us—I mean, the long myth, the myth from the waters of chaos to the Isis and Osiris myth—tells us the world began with chaos, eventually it was peopled by gods, which give you some order, we do have the good guy winning in the end. And it also tells us, if you behave properly, take the right precautions, you will be resurrected. There is a life after death. And this is a myth. So that's mythology.

But remember I said I wanted to do three things. I wanted to do mythology, I wanted to do religion, and I wanted to do philosophy. And let me say how religion differs. Religion—the same questions are handled by religion as mythology. Is there life after death? Various religions give the answer. Christianity will say yes. Judaism doesn't say anything about it. Jewish religion doesn't have anything about life after death. But the important thing about a religious belief is that, one, there is an element of faith. It involves belief. If someone says, "I believe in life after death because that's my religion," that ends it. That's the element of belief, and that's fine. But, also, we're supposed to believe religious stories in a historical way. These aren't just myths. So, for example, when Moses leads the Israelites out of Egypt, that's believed to be a historical event. Whereas in mythology, it doesn't make sense to say, what was Zeus's birthday. It does make sense to say, what was Moses's birthday. We may not know the answer, but it's a meaningful question because in religion the belief is that a character like Moses actually existed, unlike say the Greek gods on Mt. Olympus. In a sense, one man's mythology may be another person's religion. But the crucial thing is, mythology doesn't take place in historical time; religion does.

Now what about the third category I said, philosophy? Well, philosophy tries to do the same thing, answer the same questions, is there life after death? How did the universe begin? But it does it differently from either mythology or religion. Philosophy requires proof. You cannot in philosophy simply say, that's what I believe. It requires proof. Now the question is, how do you get such proof? How do you prove that there is life after death? Well, philosophers have tried. For example, René Descartes was a religious person, but he tried to prove logically that God must exist.

Now the point I want to make is a point that usually when I'm in a large classroom and I'm presenting to my students they are ready to kill me after I say what I'm going to say. But I'm going to try to make it clear that I think, maybe, hopefully you'll come around to the way I view it. Philosophical questions like, "is there life after death," "is there a God," are not matters of opinion. There is a right and wrong answer. Many people think, oh no, philosophy is just saying anything off the top of your head. No.

Now, let me try to convince you. I know a lot of you are saying, "Mmm, maybe not; I don't think so." Whether there is life after death or not is not a matter of a belief or opinion; it's a fact. Either there is life after death or there isn't. It doesn't matter whether you don't know the answer; that's different from it not being answerable. For example, we may not know how many people are in the next room, but there are either seven people in the next room or there aren't. And life after death is a question like that. We can't settle empirically, we can't observe right now, but it has an answer. So philosophical questions have answers; we shouldn't think that they don't. And they are very important.

Now, some people may be skeptical that they can be answered; that I can understand. But let me suggest that I think they can. Philosophers try to answer questions. For example, one, everybody has wondered about the beginning of the universe. I'm sure you all wondered about it. How did it begin? Well, science says the big bang, the basic theory that in the beginning everything was in a tightly balled mass, all the mass of the universe was in this thing about the size of a golf ball, then it explodes, and the rest are the laws of physics. That's not the question that philosophers ask about the beginning of the universe. The real question is, how did that golf ball get there? What was there before the golf ball?

Now as an example, to show you that these questions are answerable, and how we might proceed to answer them, and how it's different from religion, which just ends with belief, think about this, there are only two possibilities for the beginning of the universe. One is it doesn't have a beginning. As far back as you go in time there was always something. That's one possibility. The other possibility is that the universe did begin at a time and it began out of nothing. At time T-0 there was nothing. At time T-1, poof, there was something. Almost by magic, it's called *ex nihilo*, Latin, "out of nothing." Those are the only two possibilities. Either something came out of nothing or there was always something.

Now, think about it, just by this kind of simpleminded philosophical exercise, we're almost at the answer to how the universe began. We've limited it to two possibilities, and now the question is, can we eliminate one of those possibilities? Is one of those impossible? And if one of those is impossible, if we can show that then we know the other one must be true and we philosophically answered the question of how did the universe begin. Now, I'm not going to deal with which one is possible or not; I'll let you figure that out. But let me say this, philosophical questions are important and have answers.

Now what we need to know is, did the Egyptians do philosophy? There is no question about it, they did mythology. We know about their myths. Plenty of religion; we have religious texts. We don't have any philosophical texts. That is a question that people are still debating. Could a civilization as advanced as Egypt have created such masterpieces of art, such incredible works of art in temples, and not done philosophy? One possibility is, they just didn't write it down. It was so special that they didn't want to commit it to papyrus; it's a possibility, but we're not sure.

But the important thing is to get clear the differences between mythology, religion, and philosophy, and that certainly mythology and religion were a central part of the Egyptian mind.

Now, next time what I'd like to do is tell you about the beginnings of Egyptology, how we learn all this stuff. And it all began with Napoleon Bonaparte going to Egypt. So I'll see you next time.

Lecture Four
Napoleon and the Beginnings of Egyptology

Scope:

We will learn how Napoleon's Egyptian campaign of 1798–1801 began modern Egyptology. We will discuss the reasons Napoleon went to Egypt and the main events of the campaign but will focus on the corps of 150 scientists that he brought with the army. We will see how Egypt had been studied before Napoleon's expedition and contrast this with the scientific observations and reports that his savants produced. We discuss in detail the monumental publication *Description de l'Egypte* and how it set the standard for all future Egyptological publications. We conclude with the discovery of the Rosetta stone.

Outline

I. Napoleon Bonaparte had several reasons to go to Egypt.

    A. Napoleon didn't want to invade England, as the French government wanted, so he invaded Egypt instead.

    B. He hoped to cut off England's land route to India.

    C. He was following in the footsteps of Alexander the Great, a personal hero.

    D. Napoleon was also a scholar—a member of the French Institute in mathematics.

II. What was known about Egypt?

    A. Hieroglyphs were a dead language, so Egyptian history was unknown.

    B. There was no systematic study or collection of objects, merely cabinets of curiosities and missionaries' reports.

    C. Richard Pococke and Frederik Norden, sea captains, were early visitors to Egypt but untrained as observers.

III. Bonaparte assembled an all-star team of 150 scientists and artists for his campaign. His destination was a secret.

    A. Dominique-Vivant Denon (1747–1825) was an artist who became first director of the Louvre.

    B. Claude Louis Berthollet (1748–1822) was Napoleon's chemist.

C. Geoffroy Saint-Hilaire (1772–1844) was a brilliant young zoologist who went on to accomplish much.

D. Nicolas Conte had the ability to manufacture anything: "All the arts in his hands and all the sciences in his head."

E. Redoute, Dolomieu, Fourier, Monge, and others were exceptional men who rounded out an extraordinary team.

F. Students and engineers, printers and printing presses all came along for the adventure.

IV. In spite of all the intellectual baggage, there was a war to fight.

A. The Mamelukes, once bought as slaves, had become a warrior caste that tyrannized Egypt. Bonaparte promised to liberate the Egyptians, going so far as to issue proclamations that were the first printed documents in Arabic.

B. At the Battle of the Pyramids, East met the modern West for the first time. The Mameluke cavalry charged the French army, massed together in squares. The French won the battle decisively.

C. The Battle of the Nile was Napoleon's first setback.

    1. British admiral Horatio Nelson's impatience led to victory for the English.

    2. The French were anchored near the shore, their guns aimed seaward. Nelson daringly cut between ships and shore and attacked the French from the rear.

    3. The French ship *L'Orient*, the largest in the world, suddenly exploded, a sound heard twenty miles away.

    4. Felicia Hemans's famous first line, "The boy stood on the burning deck" (Admiral Casabianca's son), is about the Battle of the Nile.

    5. Many scientific instruments were lost when the ships went down, a blow to the expedition.

    6. Even worse, the French were cut off from supplies coming from the European mainland.

D. Plague began to take its toll on the French during the siege of Acre, a fort on the Mediterranean.

E. Napoleon suddenly deserted his troops and returned to France, declaring himself the "conqueror" of Egypt.

V. The campaign gave birth to modern Egyptology.

A. Scientists published the *Description de l'Egypte*, ten volumes full of drawings and illustrations. The Egyptian fad in furnishings and fashion was soon all the rage in Europe.

B. Napoleon instructed his men to copy the hieroglyphs *exactly*. This would turn out to be one of the most lasting accomplishments of the campaign.

C. Collections of antiquities and natural history were systematically framed.

VI. The Rosetta stone was the key to deciphering the hieroglyphs.

A. England, the victor, agreed by treaty that the French could retain all the discoveries of the campaign—except the antiquities.

B. The most important of these was the Rosetta stone. Scholars immediately knew it was crucial—the inscription appeared in both Greek and Egyptian. Although the French tried to retain it, today the Rosetta stone is in the British Museum instead of the Louvre because of this treaty.

Essential Reading:
J. Christopher Herold, *Bonaparte in Egypt*.

Supplementary Reading:
Bob Brier, *The Glory of Ancient Egypt*.

Questions to Consider:
1. Why did Bonaparte go to Egypt?
2. What were the contributions to Egyptology that came out of the Egyptian campaign?

Lecture Four—Transcript
Napoleon and the Beginnings of Egyptology

Hello again. Remember in the first lecture where I said we're going to do it chronologically from the beginning toward the end with a few side trips; this is a side trip.

What I'd like to talk about today is a military campaign, Napoleon's campaign in Egypt, and how it led to the beginning of modern Egyptology. Now, what I'll do is I'll explain the campaign; I'll explain why Bonaparte was going to Egypt. But I'll also explain why he took with him 150 scientists, artists, engineers. And then I'll try to show you what came out of this expedition, how modern Egyptology is really due to Napoleon Bonaparte.

But first, why did he go to Egypt? Well, 1798 is the year that he took off. At this time, Napoleon isn't the emperor; he is just a young general. He's 29 years old, and he's coming out of the Italian campaigns. He's done very well, marvelously. He is the hero. He has defeated an Italian army, he has conquered Italy, organized an army, and he's also brought back an awful lot of treasures to Paris. He has taken the artworks from Italy and brought them back to Paris, so he's the hero.

He comes back to Paris, conquering hero, 29 years old, top of the world, and the directory who was running the government says to him, your next task is to invade England. Now Bonaparte is infantry, he is not a sailor, so he doesn't want to do that, all right. England is, of course, the enemy of France at this time. He looks at the boats and says, they are inadequate, we're not going to invade England. But he has another plan. He suggests, "I'll go and conquer Egypt." Now there are several reasons why conquering Egypt is a reasonable thing for Bonaparte to say. One is, politically the worst thing you could do to England is conquer Egypt, why? This was England's land route to India. English trade depended on controlling Egypt. And if the French controlled Egypt, the English economy was dead. So he was going to strike a blow at England by going to Egypt.

The other reason he wanted to go, I think, was personal. Alexander the Great was always his hero. And Alexander the Great began his great career by conquering Egypt. And he even said, all greatness starts in the East. Napoleon wanted to conquer Egypt, I think, because Alexander the Great had done it. Now, also, I think he wanted to see the place. You know, he was a person like we are. He was also a scholar, by the way. Don't think of Napoleon as this crude guy, not at all. He was a member of the French Institute in mathematics. He was a bit of a culture vulture. Wherever he went he would draw up lists of artworks to be requisitioned. He was an okay guy. As a matter of fact, you know how our system of numbering the streets, odd number houses on one side, even numbered on the other, that was Napoleon's idea. He got lost one night, ticked off, he couldn't find a house—we're going to number odd number, even number. But Napoleon was really somebody to be reckoned with. So he was off to Egypt; the year is 1798.

Now what was known about Egypt in 1798? Not much. Hieroglyphs hadn't been deciphered yet. And remember, by the way, the word is hieroglyphs. The carvings you see on the walls are not hieroglyphics—that's an adjective—it's a hieroglyphic writing, it's a hieroglyphic script, but the ducks and birds are hieroglyphs. Hieroglyphs hadn't been deciphered, so a lot of the history was unknown. There was no systematic attempt at organizing the knowledge that was known. For example, there weren't museums with large collections of Egyptian antiquities. The closest thing to a museum collection were cabinets of curiosities. These were wealthy people in Europe, who had little cabinets, literally, like a china closet in their houses where they would have curiosities. It might be a mummy's arm brought back from Egypt by a sea captain. It might be a two-headed baby in a jar. These were the cabinets of curiosities that wealthy people—you would come and after dinner, "let me show you my cabinet." So this was as close to a museum collection as we had. So Bonaparte was sailing off into sort of uncharted waters; he was really doing something new.

Now, also, the information that had been gained about Egypt came from unprofessional sources. What I mean by that is, you get missionaries going to do missionary work and they'd come back and report. They weren't trained observers. They had their own agendas. So you don't often get an objective reporting. Or sometimes it will be a sea captain who sailed up the Nile and would describe what he saw. In 1737 two sea captains went to Egypt—one by the name of Pococke, the other Norton (Norton was Danish and Pococke was English). We don't know that they even talked to each other. They were in Egypt at the same time, and I figured out their ships probably crossed in the Nile. But each one wrote a description of Egypt, and what you get are kind of drawings that are unprofessional. I mean, Norton's look like he never left the ship. There were little tiny pyramids across the water, and it's almost like he never got off his boat. So you never had a really good description of this country Egypt that Napoleon was sailing for.

Bonaparte was going to change all that. He took with him 150 artists, scientists, and it was an all-star team. Now let me say this, it wasn't easy to recruit these guys. Why? His destination was a secret. When he sailed from France in 1798, he took 55,000 soldiers with him, and practically none of them knew where they were going. Incredible, but true. Only the captains, of course, of the ships of the fleet knew. He kept it a secret, and many of the scientists didn't know where they were going. They were merely recruited for a great experience. So when they sailed there was a lot of rumor. Some people thought, well, maybe we're going to the Holy Land, which was close, but nobody knew for sure. They started at Malta, by the way. They had stopped along the way at Malta, to conquer it, because Malta was strategically important, and there are great stories about what happened. Malta was controlled by the knights of Malta, but they were an old kind of rusty organization. They were old men who didn't really want to fight. And it took two days and Napoleon was in control of Malta. He quickly took all the treasures of the knights of Malta, which included, by the way, life-size silver statues, twelve of them, of the apostles. They've never been seen again. They disappeared. The only thing he left for the knights was a splinter from the true cross; that's what he left them.

But after Malta, he sailed for Egypt with his all-star crew. Now let me tell you about some of these guys. Vivant Denon was probably the second oldest member of the group. They were young. He was in his fifties, Denon, but he was a professional artist and a friend of Bonaparte, and he is later going to become the first director of the Louvre and the first to work on the Museum when it's founded. It first started out as the Museum Napoleon, by the way. Denon went along as an artist, but there was also Berthollet, the chemist. And Napoleon had known him before, and he called him "my chemist." He also took along guys like Geoffrey Saint-Hilaire who was a great naturalist, young, up and coming. You know who else was there, the mathematician, Fourier, as in the Fourier transformations; he was there. The mineralogist, Dolomieu, after whom we have the mineral dolomite named; he was there. There was Monge, who was a great mathematician. It was an amazing crew. Even Redoute, who was a brother of the famous Redoute who painted roses, to do the botanical drawings. He was going to describe all of Egypt.

Now along with this sort of senior scientists, and most of them were professors, came a younger crew of students. Now these guys were professors at the École Polytechnique, for example, so they brought with them students. You know, "Hey, I'm going on ... you're 19 years old ... come on, we're going." And you would have young students along. So many of the people there were like 17, 18. I mean, there is even one kid who took his books along—he was 17 years old when he left—took his books along, studied in Cairo, and the next year he was examined and he became an engineer. He graduated in Cairo. So it was an exciting adventure for the savants.

But there was a war to fight. Napoleon still had to conquer Egypt. So he leaves in 1798, conquers Malta, and then there is a war to fight. Now he lands his men near Alexandria, all is well. But one of the things about this campaign that sort of reveals Bonaparte's personality—he was always impatient. I mean, he was a genius, and he was brilliant, but he was impatient. They landed in August, summer, it's hot, they have woolen uniforms and no canteens. They had not prepared for a desert campaign. And the first thing they do when they march from Alexandria to Cairo, the desert road, they start dying of thirst. The locals had filled in the wells, so there was no water. Men shot themselves they were in such agony. Now Bonaparte when he landed was trying to explain to the people, "I'm a friend; I'm not going to conquer."

Now understand the political situation in Egypt at the time. Egypt was not being ruled by the Egyptians per se. The Turks had official control of Egypt. And the Turks had as their kind of janissaries, their emissaries in Egypt, the Mamelukes. Now "mameluke" is a word that means "bought man." The Mamelukes were originally bought as slaves from the Circassian mountains as young boys, and they were trained to be soldiers in Egypt. Eventually they revolted; they became soldiers, revolted. And now the Mamelukes were in charge, and they were tyrannizing the peasants, taxing them heavily. And Bonaparte lands and he issues a proclamation to the Egyptians: "We come here to free you." Now, remember, this is just after the French Revolution. We're talking *liberté, egalité, fraternité*, and that's what he's preaching to these people. He says, "We're going to liberate you from the Turks."

Interesting, by the way, the very first document ever published in Arabic in Egypt was Napoleon's proclamation. He brought the printing presses, the first Arabic printing presses, to Egypt. And where did he get the typeface? They raided the Vatican. They went to the Vatican, took all the typeface, brought it over with printing presses, with two printers, and they were set up to print. So the first documents to get published in Arabic were by Napoleon.

But anyway, we've got to get to the war. They marched to Cairo, eventually they make it. Men kill themselves; it's a terrible situation. And they are just about hanging on by their fingernails, and they are about to fight the battle of their lives—the battle of the pyramids. There are two major battles fought in Egypt—the battle of the pyramids and the battle of the Nile. Neither one is accurate; they are both misnamed. The battle of the pyramids was not by the pyramids and the battle of the Nile was not by the Nile. But we'll get to the battle of the Nile in a minute.

The battle of the pyramids was fought in a melon patch, about six or seven miles from the pyramids in a place now called Inbaba; there is a camel market there now. But you could see the pyramids in the distance. And the Mamelukes had been massing their forces. So you're looking to get a clash for the first time in history of a modern Western fighting army, Napoleon's, with an Eastern fighting force, but they were very, very different. The Mamelukes were all cavalry. The typical Mameluke—and these were, I mean, really great looking guys. They had turbans, they had flowing robes, they all had these wonderful horses. They all had two pistols, swords, and a servant or two running behind. So what they would do is they would go into battle with their horses, with their pistols, fire their pistols, throw them over their shoulders, the servants would grab them, reload them, find them in the battle, give them back their pistols, and it would all continue again. So we were going to get these very brave Mamelukes, skilled horsemen, fighting Napoleon's disciplined army. A lot of these guys had been with him in Italy and knew it worked; they had never lost. Napoleon had never lost a battle.

So the battle of the pyramids is about to be fought. Napoleon has his men form squares. You would have riflemen on the outside. You have artillery on the corners, and the cavalry inside the square. The

Mamelukes are about to charge. Probably about, I mean, more than 5,000, we're not sure of the exact numbers, because they get exaggerated, but certainly more than 5,000. Napoleon's squares are formed, and just before the battle Napoleon points to the pyramids; you can see them in the distance. And he says, "Soldiers, from these heights 40 centuries of history look down upon you." The remarkable thing is he was about right; the pyramids were about 40 centuries old. And you wonder how he knew it, because remember, it hadn't been studied yet. It was really an educated guess.

And the battle began. It was quickly over. The Mamelukes charged and the squares held their fire until the Mamelukes were right on top of them and they just blew them away. The Mamelukes retreated, massed again, another charge, and it was clear they were no match for a Western army. The Mamelukes were done with.

Now the army was quite happy about this, not just because they won the battle, but these Mamelukes carried their wealth with them. They often had gold coins sewn into their turbans. So right after the battle there was a tremendous amount of looting. The Mamelukes were on the battlefield dead and they had swords inlaid with gold, they had pistols that were fantastic. So the army did quite well. And now Napoleon was in charge of Cairo. He had conquered.

But his victory wasn't going to last very long, because let me tell you what happened with the next battle, the battle of the Nile. Napoleon establishes himself quickly in Cairo. He takes over the houses of the Mamelukes. Things are going well. And then comes Horatio Nelson, the English admiral, who had been looking for Napoleon's fleet. Now, nobody really knew where Napoleon was going, so they had been searching around. They heard he had been in Malta; they tried other places.

Napoleon had had his fleet anchored at Abukir Bay. The Admiral, Admiral Brueys, had suggested don't anchor here; it's not good protection. Let's take the fleet away to Corfu; they wanted to go away from Egypt. Bonaparte was an infantryman, didn't understand how you flee away from where you need the army. He said, no, anchor here. So Brueys did a smart thing. He anchored as close to shore as he could so nobody finding him could go between him and the shore. And he pointed all his guns seaward, so if an attack came from the sea, from the Mediterranean, he could fire. Thirteen ships of the line, they are called; those are the fighting ships, not the transport ships. There were thirteen ships of the line anchored in Abukir Bay.

And Nelson sails into Abukir Bay and sees them just lined up. Now Nelson did two things that had never been done in the history of naval warfare. The first thing was when he sees them it's about four o'clock in the afternoon. It's going to get dark fairly soon and naval battles are not fought at night; at least they weren't then. Normally you would wait for the next day. Not Nelson, boom, sails right in and starts the battle. So you know the battle is going to be mostly at night. The next thing he does is he sails in between the ships and the shore, something that was thought impossible. He had no charts of that shore; he had no idea how deep the water was. But he told his men, go right in, and they made it, they could do it. So now you've got the ships between the French and the shore, the British are there, all the guns are pointed seaward, and those French ships are sitting ducks. They can't turn the guns. It's not an era when you can turn a canon around very easily.

Napoleon's entire fleet was destroyed in one day. The battle went through the night. The largest ship in the history of the world at that point was the *L'Orient*, Napoleon's flagship. When that ship blew up it was heard 20 miles away. It's a famous, famous explosion. When the ship blew up everybody was so shocked that the fighting stopped for ten minutes. They just kind of didn't believe it. It was at night; it was dark.

Also, some of you may remember, some of you maybe are old enough to remember a poem that I had to learn when I was a kid. It begins, "The boy stood on the burning deck." That is about a young boy who was the captain's son, Casabianca's son, who when the ship blew up he refused to leave the ship because his father wasn't there and he went down with the ship. That's about the Egyptian campaign.

So Bonaparte now, his fleet is destroyed. He is stranded in Egypt. Nelson, he's a naval man, he's not military, he's not an infantry guy. Nelson says Bonaparte is in a fix that he's not going to get out of, and he simply sailed away leaving Bonaparte stranded. He couldn't get reinforcements, he couldn't get new supplies, he was in trouble. Didn't faze Bonaparte.

What does he do? He founds an institute to study Egypt. His fleet is gone; he founds this institute. Now, fortunately, one of the people with him was a guy named Conté. Conté was a guy who could do anything; he was an engineer. And what Bonaparte once said of him was, he has all the arts in his hands and all the science in his head. Now when the ships went down, they lost a lot of equipment, surveying equipment, scientific instruments, all kinds of things. Conté could make it. He could recreate almost anything. So Conté helped and they set up workshops and all that. And the amazing thing is, as this war is going on, the 150 scientists are going about their job of studying Egypt. They are drawing plants. They are studying animals. They are uncovering Egypt.

Now it's a good thing that they had Conté, because when Bonaparte came into Egypt there were no places where you could buy things like microscopes, telescopes. They had silk bazaars; that's what they had. So they are doing the best they can. Now Bonaparte heads out for another battle. He heads out to Acre, which was in Syria then; today it's in modern day Israel. And this is the battle when Napoleon suffers his first real loss, Napoleon himself. Abukir was a disaster, but it wasn't his baby.

Acre was controlled by a man named Djzer Pasha. Now "*djzer*" means "the butcher." He was called the butcher because he was not a nice man. I'll give you an example. Djzer had a physician whose name was Hiam the Jew, and Hiam was asked to examine one of Djzer's wives to find out if—the woman was pregnant—to find out if the wife was going to have a boy or girl. Now how was Hiam going to do this? He wasn't even allowed to examine the woman. She would put her hand through a hole in the wall, he would look at her hand, and he had to tell Djzer whether it was a boy or a girl. So Hiam took a guess. Djzer, anxious to find out, had the woman brought and cut open so he could see whether the fetus was a boy or a girl. Hiam guessed wrong and lost an ear, and eventually lost an eye. Djzer was not a nice person.

Now Napoleon was going to do battle with Djzer. And it's at the fort of Acre where he loses this battle. Now understand that Acre is on the water; it's a fort. And the way you normally take a fort is either by starving it out—you camp around it, don't let it get supplies—or you siege it, you charge, make a breach in the wall, and go in. They couldn't starve it out because it's on the water and the British were supplying Djzer Pasha with supplies, so that wouldn't work. So Napoleon had to siege the fort. But he didn't wait for his canons to come up, and they kept charging the fort. The men would die; it was a terrible, terrible situation for the French army.

And not only were they losing the battle because of Djzer Pasha being reinforced and just shooting canon at them one after the other, the plague had struck. The French started dying of the plague, bubonic plague. So they were really fighting two battles, the military one and this medical one. Now while this is going on, as I say, the scientists are recording all of Egypt, a remarkable thing, 150 men doing the best they can.

Now, by 1798, Napoleon knew he was defeated. He marches back from Acre. Comes in victorious, by the way, he marches victoriously into Cairo. They get the healthy ones in front, they march in, they say, yes, we conquered. Comes in, always spinning his own legend. But Bonaparte knew it was over. It's now 1799 and he's making plans to leave. Bonaparte does not tell his men. He leaves a letter for General Kléber, his next in charge, and it says, "By the time you read this I'll be on a ship heading for Paris. There are developments in France that call me. I must leave." Kléber is really ticked off. I mean, he's got a losing war. But Bonaparte left with Denon, the artist, and a few other people. And what does he do when he returns? He declares himself a hero. He has medals struck showing that he is the conqueror of Egypt. He's founded an institute. He's come back, and he has medals struck saying, "I've conquered Egypt." I mean, it's amazing. The British knew the truth, though, and they had cartoons, wonderful cartoons of Napoleon's scientists studying crocodiles. I mean, there is one great one that shows one of the scientists being bitten by a crocodile and the book that is falling out of his arm says, "Le droits de crocodiles," "The rights of crocodiles." And it's sort of a way of putting that while this war is going on these guys have got their heads in another world. But it was the beginning of modern Egyptology. Even though Napoleon is declaring himself the hero returning, and he's not the hero, lots of things are going to happen.

When they get back, eventually, there is a truce in 1801. The scientists are going to return and they are going to publish what is probably the greatest publication in the history of the world up till then, *Description de l'Egypte*. It's ten huge volumes of engravings. It's the first time that the West saw Egypt accurately depicted. It's fantastic. It shows the temples; it shows everything. This is the first time that the West is going to realize that pyramids aren't that pointy. Now always you had people describing things who hadn't even seen it, doing drawings. The *Description de l'Egypte* showed it all.

Not only that, they brought back collections. These guys were professionals, they were artists, they were engineers who could measure and draw carefully. They brought back collections of antiquities that had never been assembled. It was the first coherent attempt at assembling a collection. I mean, it's remarkable what they did.

Now when the *Description de l'Egypte* was published, it was a sensation. People started a fad that we call Egyptomania. For example, furniture started to have legs in the shape of mummies, wrapped up mummies. And women used to wear their hairdos, they called it *à la Egyptienne*, in what they felt were Egyptian ways.

But it was also important for the zoologists. They had brought back their specimens. Now it's an amazing story how these guys ever got their specimens back. Think about it, they had lost a war. When the British came in 1801 to work out the treaty the deal was the following: All antiquities go back to England. Everything the French had collected was British property; that was the treaty. The scientists all said—now these are guys who had spent two years under horrible conditions collecting their birds, collecting the plants, collecting everything they wanted. The scientists, the zoologists, the botanists, they all said, "We'd rather go back to England with our collections then lose them." They weren't going to let their collections go.

Now the British were really quite decent about it. They said, "No, you can take your collections with you," and they let the French go back with their collections. It was really a rather magnanimous thing. And this became the beginnings of modern collections for museums. When museums would send out expeditions to collect, this is where it all comes from. I mean, think how audacious it was for Bonaparte, going off to fight a war, and what does he do, in addition he takes 150 scientists and says, oh, we're going to do a scientific study. He was going to colonize Egypt. That was his intention. It was going to become a French colony. So, really from Bonaparte's military campaign, we're starting to see the beginnings, just the beginnings of modern Egyptology.

Now, let me say something about how they made the recordings. As I said before, the ancient Egyptian language was a dead language; nobody could read it, nobody. As a matter of fact, nobody even thought that it contained any history, that it might contain records of the kings, that it might contain annals of military expeditions. Nobody ever thought that. It was always believed to be purely religious. Because think about the name, hieroglyphs, *hiero*, "sacred," *glyphs*, "carvings." Because only the priests could read them in Egypt, that was the literary class. So everybody thought these were just religious texts.

But Bonaparte had instructed his men, the scientists—some of them were linguists—he had instructed them to copy the hieroglyphs accurately. And there were many men who did nothing but copy hieroglyphs, and they had done so accurately. I can pick up a page of the *Description de l'Egypte*, I can pick up the page, and I can look at the hieroglyphs and I can read them, and they didn't know what they were copying. So it's really quite a remarkable achievement. And that is perhaps one of the most lasting things that Bonaparte achieved. The decipherment of hieroglyphs is going to come right out of this expedition, and let me tell you how.

The English said, "Okay, you can keep the birds, you can keep the plants, but all the antiquities, they're ours," and that included one of the most crucial of all antiquities that Bonaparte's men found—the Rosetta stone, the famous Rosetta stone. It was found at a fort in the town of Rosetta, Rashid, as it was called then, found in the town of Rashid. And it was an interesting finding. It was found by a man named Bouchard, Lieutenant Bouchard. Everybody was looking for the decipherment of hieroglyphs; everybody knew that maybe this expedition would lead to the decipherment of hieroglyphs.

But when they found the Rosetta stone they knew immediately that this was going to be the key to decipherment. Why? Because it had the same inscription in two different languages. It had it in Egyptian, but it also had it in Greek. And the Greek inscription said, it's the same inscription twice, right, actually three times, but I'll talk about that later. So the Rosetta stone was going to be the key to the decipherment of hieroglyphs. Bouchard found it, it was brought to Cairo, the savants looked at it and said, this is going to be the key. The scientists knew this was going to be the key.

But the treaty said all the antiquities have to come to England. The French desperately tried to keep the Rosetta stone, desperately. The general who was now in charge, remember Bonaparte leaves, puts Kléber in charge. Kléber is assassinated soon after. And General Menou is now in charge and Menou says, "This is not part of the government's property; this is my personal property, so therefore you shouldn't have it." The English simply pointed a canon at his head and said, "We're taking it." And that is why today the Rosetta stone is not in the Louvre in Paris; it's in the British Museum in England, because Napoleon lost that campaign.

And the Rosetta stone was going to be the key. Fortunately, fortunately, the French had made copies of the Rosetta stone. They used it—it's inscribed, it's a stone that has carvings. So they used it as a printing stone. They inked it and ran paper over it and pressed it so that they had impressions of it. And scientists are scientists; they are not interested in war; they are not interested in nationality; they passed out copies to everybody who wanted it. So the French had copies of the Rosetta stone, at least, and this is what would lead to the decipherment of hieroglyphs and it's all because of Napoleon Bonaparte.

Now, next time we're going to talk about the Rosetta stone and about actual decipherment of ancient Egyptian. See you next time.

Lecture Five
The Rosetta Stone, and Much More

Scope:

This lecture has three distinct goals: (1) The student will learn why the Rosetta stone was the key to deciphering the ancient Egyptian language. (2) The student will learn the four different scripts in which ancient Egyptian was written (hieroglyphic, hieratic, demotic, and Coptic). (3) The student will see the three different ways that hieroglyphic signs could be used.

Outline

I. Ancient Egyptian was a dead language.

    A. Because Egypt had long been occupied by foreigners, including the Greeks and Romans, the ancient written language had expired. It remained dead for over 1,000 years.

    B. The central assumption was that the ancient language was ideographic, not alphabetic. But this was wrong. The ancient Greek writer Horapollo correctly asserted that the mysterious symbols represented something other than what they depicted, although he was wrong in other matters.

II. The Rosetta stone was the key to decipherment.

    A. The stone was found in the foundations of a fort at Rosetta and is stela-shaped, like a tombstone. Stelae were carved stones with inscriptions that were placed like bulletin boards in front of temples.

    B. The stone contained three scripts (hieroglyphic, demotic, and Greek) but only two languages (Greek and Egyptian).

        1. The hieroglyphic script was used for sacred texts.

        2. More efficient than hieroglyphs, demotic was a script the people wrote.

        3. Greek, the third script, was the language of the rulers of Egypt during the period that the stone was composed. The significance of its appearance on the stone was realized immediately through the last line: "Written in sacred and native and Greek characters."

        4. Hieratic was not on the Rosetta stone but was a cursive, shorthand form of hieroglyphs.

> **5.** Coptic, an ancient form of Egyptian spelled out in the Greek alphabet, was not on the Rosetta stone either but was instrumental in deciphering it.

C. The Rosetta stone was taken by the British in 1801. Contrary to popular belief, it is reddish granite, not black basalt.

D. The stone's decipherment was the product of several minds.

> **1.** Thomas Young, an English physician, correctly concluded that the sign for "Ptolemy," for example, was phonetic—that an alphabet, not an ideogram, was at work.

> **2.** Jean Francois Champollion, a Frenchman who knew Coptic, translated the message in 1822 through his knowledge of ancient Egyptian sounds. Coptic, then, proved to be our connection with spoken ancient Egyptian.

III. The ancient Egyptian language works on several levels.

A. There are several kinds of hieroglyphs.

> **1.** Hieroglyphs can be phonetic, like our alphabet. In ancient Egyptian, a rectangle represents a *p*; a hand represents a *d*. As in many ancient languages, there were no vowels.

> **2.** Determinatives clarify the meaning of such phonetic words. They are placed at the end of a word as an ideographic reminder.

> **3.** Ideograms, or pictorial writing, represent concepts. These images were a shorthand version of hieroglyphs.

B. Hieroglyphs could be written left to right, right to left, or top to bottom. For purposes of symmetry, which the Egyptians admired, the language was thus very flexible.

C. You can easily write your own name in hieroglyphs through transliteration.

Essential Reading:

Stephen Quirke and Carol Andrews, *The Rosetta Stone.*

Supplementary Reading:

Mark Collier and Bill Manley, *How to Read Hieroglyphs.*

Questions to Consider:

1. What three scripts are on the Rosetta stone?

2. Why did ancient Egyptian become a dead language?

Lecture Five—Transcript
The Rosetta Stone, and Much More

Hello again. Let me do a brief summary of what we did last time, because it leads directly into what I want to do today. Remember we talked about Napoleon's campaign when he went off to Egypt. And how he didn't just go for a military expedition; he took with him 150 scientists to study Egypt as it had never been studied before. No one had ever done anything like that.

Now, what his campaign would be was a military disaster. He lost badly, but modern Egyptology came out of it. And in particular we're most grateful for the Rosetta stone, and that's what I want to talk about today. And I have a specific goal today. I'm even going to give you a little bit of homework, but don't worry, it's easy. Today I want you to understand why the Rosetta stone was the key to the decipherment of ancient Egyptian language. And I want you to know the different scripts that ancient Egyptian was written in. It was written in hieroglyphic script, what's called a hieratic script, a demotic script, a Coptic script—all words that you probably haven't heard, but that's okay. By the end of the lesson I think you'll understand them quite well, and my prediction is and my goal is that every one of you will be able to read and write your own name in hieroglyphs by the end of this lecture. So let's see if it works.

Now let me first explain why ancient Egyptian became a dead language. Toward the end of Egypt's long history, 3,000 years of historic records, toward the end, Egypt was conquered by many foreign lands. And we'll talk about those later—the Assyrians, the Libyans, the Babylonians, the Nubians, toward the very end the Greeks, and then finally the Romans. And because Egypt was eventually occupied by foreigners, the language died out. At one point Greek became the major language of commerce. Then the Romans took over. So by 425 A.D. we have the last inscription written on a wall in a temple in ancient Egyptian. That is the last time that we know that anybody could read or write ancient Egyptian; it was probably a priest.

So after 425 A.D. no one could read ancient Egyptian records. And it remained a dead language; it remained a dead language for over a thousand years. Now, why? The answer is that everybody was making the same false assumption, that it was picture writing. Now think about it. Don't most people think of hieroglyphs as picture writing? That when you see birds and feet, like maybe you see feet walking and it's talking about somebody going somewhere perhaps, and when you see birds it's talking about birds, and when you see snakes it's talking about snakes. No, that's wrong.

Ancient Egyptian was basically an alphabetic language like ours. But everybody was assuming it was picture writing, so nobody was deciphering it. Interesting, by the way, think about this, if it really were picture writing, wouldn't we all be able to read it? Right, we would all be able to read it. But no, it's not picture writing; it's mainly alphabetic. So for over a thousand years nobody could read or write it. There was a lot of speculation, I'll tell you that much.

One Greek writer, who had an interesting name, Horapollo, Horus and Apollo combined in Greek, wrote a treatise about ancient Egyptian hieroglyphs, but he couldn't read them; he had no idea. It's an interesting treatise. He got some things right, some things wrong. I'll give you an example. He says—this is right, this is the right part—he says that a duck, when you see the hieroglyph of a duck, it was used by the ancient Egyptians to indicate someone's son, S-O-N, the child, that a duck represented a son. He was right. The reason he gave was, thinking it's picture writing, because the ducks fight so fiercely for their offspring, the duck was associated with children. That was really wrong. The duck indeed did represent a child, a male child. But the reason the duck represented it was that hieroglyph— and remember it's a hieroglyph, not a hieroglyphic—that hieroglyph, this picture for duck, merely is there because it's pronounced S-A, the duck represents a sound, *sa*, and that was the ancient Egyptian word for son. So when you look at a duck, when an Egyptian looked at a duck he wasn't thinking about a duck, he was thinking about the sound *sa* and that meant a male child. So Horapollo had some right, some wrong, but there was an awful lot of speculation about what these sacred carvings meant. But nobody really knew.

Now the Rosetta stone, as you'll remember from last time, it was found at a fort, Fort Rosetta. Napoleon's men were digging the fortifications, and buried into the wall of the fort was this stone, the Rosetta stone. So whoever had built the fort originally took this old stone that was around, a good piece of building material, recycled it, and put it inside the wall. Bouchard, the lieutenant who found it, was an educated man, saw there was Greek on it, saw there was ancient

Egyptian; he knew this was going to be the key. And as I said last time, it was sent down to Cairo and the scientists started studying it.

Now, first your trivia question, your Egyptological trivia question: How many languages on the Rosetta stone? You've all heard of the Rosetta stone, and I bet in high school you were taught, and I bet you were taught three. That's wrong; the answer is only two. There are three scripts on the Rosetta stone, but only two languages—Egyptian and Greek. Those are the languages. But the Egyptian is written in two scripts.

You know what it's like. We have say printing, printed letters, Latin letters, we call them, and cursive writing, when we are writing a letter. That's what the Egyptians had also, they had different forms of writing, and on the Rosetta stone are three different scripts. We have one, which is hieroglyphic, the hieroglyphic script. These are the hieroglyphs. These are the symbols that are recognizable as ducks and birds; this is what you can tell. Now, in addition the Egyptians had other scripts. One was called demotic. That's also on the Rosetta stone. Now demotic, again, comes from the Greek, it means *demos*, "the people." This is the people's writing. So in other words, hieroglyphs, the sacred carvings are used by the priests for religious texts and also used for official big statements by the pharaoh; when you put something on a temple wall about a victory, that was in hieroglyphs. But if you were writing say a laundry list or a grocery list or a receipt for goats, you did it in demotic. Because it takes a long time to draw a bird and then a foot and then—so they had a quick way of writing it, at the end of the Egyptian civilization, called demotic, so that also was on the Rosetta stone.

Now, the third script and the second language was Greek, and that's one that scholars could read at the time. And the key was the last sentence of the Greek. It says, and I'll read it to you, "Written in sacred and native and Greek characters." In other words, that last line of the Greek inscription said, "We've written the same message three ways—in sacred, hieroglyphic; native, meaning the people's writing, the demotic; and Greek." So it was the same message written three different ways in two different languages; this was going to be the key to deciphering it.

Let me say this, there were other forms of Egyptian writing. There is one other important one for us called hieratic, right again, sacred writing. This is a more cursive form of writing also. It's something in between demotic and hieroglyphs. So, for example, instead of writing the full bird you might just write its head and then its tail feathers. So it's a quicker way of writing. So you have different scripts. You have the fancy one, hieroglyphs, which takes the longest; you have hieratic, which is pretty fast; and demotic, which is really fast.

There is even one more script in Egyptian history, and let me tell you about that one, because it's going to be the key to the decipherment of hieroglyphs—Coptic. Now, Coptic comes from the Greek word. Eventually it comes from the Greek word for Egypt, *Aegyptos*, and *Aegyptos* became Copt, and that's Coptic. The Copts in Egypt, and they are there today—to this day you have Copts in Egypt— are the Christians, the Christian Egyptians. In the first century A.D., Saint Mark came into Egypt preaching the trinity. Now he was spreading Christianity, and the Egyptians adopted it very easily, for two reasons.

One is, first of all, almost all the Egyptian gods come in threes, in trinities. For example, in the town of Memphis there was a trinity of the god Ptah, his wife Sekhmet, who was a lionheaded goddess, and they have a child called Nefertum, who was a lotus god, comes out on a lotus. So they come in trinities—you have a father, mother and a son, in Memphis those three. In Thebes, in the south of Egypt, you have another three. You have Amun, who starts out as the hidden one, remember, in the primordial waters; his wife Mut, who also has a lion head; and they have a child Khonsu, a ram-headed god. Another trinity.

So Saint Mark comes in and says I'm preaching a trinity—the Egyptians were ready. There is another reason why the Egyptians could adopt the Christian trinity. The Egyptians had a history of polytheism, believing in many gods. They never felt they really had to choose. One of the things that people forget is that monotheism, the belief in one god, is divisive. If you believe in one god, then it's really: I'm right and those who don't believe are wrong. So monotheism in a sense is divisive. Polytheism, if you can believe in lots of gods, it's a lot easier in a way. And the Egyptians never felt they had to choose and pick and throw out gods. So Saint Mark came in, he said, "I've got a trinity," they said fine. And they adopted the trinity. So these people who converted are called the Copts, from *Aegyptos*.

Now, their language is Coptic. But here is where it gets interesting. Saint Mark comes in with Christianity, he says, okay you guys, you've got to change your religion, going over to Christianity. We've got a new trinity for you, but you can't use these pagan hieroglyphs anymore for our Christian religion. So the Egyptians— they are still speaking Egyptian, but they are not allowed to write their language in hieroglyphs—they need a new script. It happens at this time the Greeks had been in Egypt for many years, centuries; they ruled for three centuries. So Greek was around as a language, and they chose to write their ancient Egyptian language in the Greek alphabet. So Coptic is really ancient Egyptian written in the Greek alphabet, just kind of spelled out phonetically. That's the last script that we have of ancient Egyptian. Coptic, of course, doesn't appear on the Rosetta stone, but as you will see, it is the key to deciphering hieroglyphs. Coptic is going to be what does it.

So now we've gone through the different scripts that ancient Egyptian was written in. Hieroglyphic for the fancy religious text and official things; hieratic if it's a little bit faster, it has to be written; demotic, language of the people, written very quickly. And we have Coptic, the language of the Egyptians during the Christian period, written in Greek.

Now, the decipherment. As you remember from last time, the Rosetta stone was taken by the British. They won the war, and the Rosetta stone is in the British Museum today. You could all visit it. I'll tell you something neat, by the way, that the curator, a friend of mine, Harry James, who used to be the curator, did. It's a stone, it's a large stone, it's about this big, maybe three feet high, solid. By the way, it isn't black. It isn't black. Everybody thought it was black for 200 years. It's not, it's kind of red. And it's not basalt, which everybody thought; it's granite. Recently, the last couple of years they were cleaning it. It had gotten kind of dirty, and as they cleaned it they realized there was an awful lot of black ink on it, perhaps from the original inking of the stone when they were making the copies. But then they discovered underneath it was pinkish, and it's not really black like everyone thought. It's pink Aswan granite; it comes from a quarry in Aswan. They even figured out where the quarry is. So it's not basalt.

But anyway, my friend, Harry James, who used to be the curator at the Egyptian wing of the museum, decided that everybody should be able to touch the Rosetta stone. It's kind of neat to be able to touch a bit of history; it's a hard stone, it's not going to hurt it. So it's on display with no glass covering it, and you're allowed to touch it. You can really touch a bit of history there, but it's in the British Museum. But it is going to be, as you will see, the key to the decipherment of hieroglyphs.

Let me say this: Who deciphered the Rosetta stone, and the hieroglyphic language, and Egyptian language in general is a bit of a conjecture. People argue still about it. The main decipherer, there is no question, is a Frenchman, Champollion, and I'll tell you about him in a minute. But he didn't do it by himself. An Englishman really started the job, Thomas Young. And the British like to say that Thomas Young deciphered the Rosetta stone. So let me tell you about their contributions, and you can decide for yourself.

Thomas Young was an amazing genius. He was a physician, trained as a physician, who also came up with a theory of light, studied light, a physicist, but he loved languages, that's what he loved most. And as his escape, he set it as his task to decipher ancient Egyptian language. And when the Rosetta stone was found, he started working. Now, his first big leap was 1798, someone had suggested that the kings in Egypt wrote their names in ovals. They had seen ovals carved on the walls with hieroglyphs inside the oval, and they thought that there were the kings' names inside. They didn't know for sure; they couldn't read it. But they thought it appeared about right to have a king's name; it was long enough for a name.

So there was a suggestion that the kings' names were written in ovals. And they are called *cartouches* to this day. You know why? Because of Napoleon's expedition. When the men saw these ovals they said they looked like bullets, standing on their end, a bullet, imagine a bullet as an oval kind of with a line in the bottom. And they said, that's a *cartouche*, that's the French word for bullet. So that's why we call them *cartouches* today, because of Napoleon's soldiers.

Now, it had been suggested that the cartouches contained the names of the kings. Thomas Young figured names can't be picture writing. You can't have a picture, for example, of King Ptolemy. Now understand this, we have the Greek text on the bottom. And the first line of the Greek text, very first line, first two words, *Ptolemaios Basilios*, King Ptolemy. So the Greek let us know Ptolemy's name is on the Rosetta stone. Young figured, in the cartouche those are going to be letters of Ptolemy's name. And he started thinking it out, he said, oh, there is a little rectangle, that's a hieroglyph; that must be the "P." There is a semi-circle; that must be the "T." There is a loop, like a lasso; that must be the "O." There is an owl, might be an "M," or a stand—there are two ways of writing the "M." And he went through it and he worked out the name *Ptolemaios*, the Greek version of Ptolemy. So Thomas Young is one of the first ones to say, you've got an alphabet here, we can figure out the names.

Now, often it is said, by the way, that Cleopatra's name is on the Rosetta stone; it's not, only Ptolemy's appears. Later they found another inscription with Cleopatra's name and they used that, too. But the important thing to remember is Young figures out, "Ah ha, we've got an alphabet just like ours."

Then enter Jean Francois Champollion. Champollion was an amazing kid, and I mean kid. His father was a librarian, and Champollion was used to playing in the stacks, in the books. And always as a little kid, as he was even crawling around, he was looking at different languages on the spines of the books, trying to understand what they were, and he became almost obsessed with languages. By the time he was like 14 or 15 he knew eight languages. One of the languages that he knew was Coptic. Coptic had survived. You see Copts still existed in Egypt and they have a church, the Coptic Church. And if you go to a Coptic church, sometimes I, when I'm in Egypt, I often do it, I'll stop into a Coptic church and listen to the service. Because when you hear it, you're hearing ancient Egyptian. They've kept the language right through. So Coptic is really our connection with spoken ancient Egyptian. And Champollion knew Coptic.

Now, think about this, Thomas Young says it's an alphabet, great. So we can look at the hieroglyphs and know how it sounded. But that doesn't tell us what it means. For example, you know the hieroglyph that everybody is familiar with, *ankh*, it's like a cross, it has the loop at the top, comes down, cross bar, that's an *ankh*, people often wear them as good luck symbols. Everybody knew that that was pronounced *ankh*. The ancient Egyptians pronounced it *ankh*; from the alphabet we can figure that out. But how do you know that the ancient Egyptians meant by *ankh* the word life? It's the concept life. The answer is, in the Coptic Church's liturgy; we know that *ankh* means life. So, from Coptic, by knowing Coptic, Champollion could look at the hieroglyphs, say it's an alphabet, say it out loud, ankh, and then realize, "Ah, Coptic has that word, *ankh*, that means life." So that was the connecting thing that enabled Champollion to decipher hieroglyphs, not just phonetically but get at the meaning of it. And he was the first one to translate the Rosetta stone.

It didn't come easy, by the way. The Rosetta stone, discovered in 1799 during the campaign, brought to England in 1801, was not deciphered until 1822, 1822. It was a long haul, but he finally did it. And for the first time the records of ancient Egypt could be read thanks to Napoleon and Champollion.

Now, what I'd like to do is to show you how, just how the language worked. But let me explain what was on the Rosetta stone. You know, what's on it, what does it say? First, the Rosetta stone is what we call a stela. A stela is simply a large stone, usually three, maybe five, sometimes nine feet high, shaped like a tombstone. They are always rounded at the top, and I really do think that we get our tombstones from that. I think that's where we get the tombstone from. And these were placed in front of temples, again, kind of like a bulletin board. If you wanted to announce something, if you wanted to say something great was done, you had a stela carved. And the Rosetta stone, broken as it is, fragmented as is—it's broken, it's not complete—was originally from a stela, it was a large stone erected in front of a temple.

Now, it was erected during the reign of King Ptolemy V—a Greek who was ruling Egypt toward the end of Egyptian civilization. Now, Ptolemy had done a couple of nice things for the priests. He said, you don't have to pay certain kinds of taxes, you don't have to make this trip that you always have to make to deposit your taxes. And the priests were very thankful. So what they did was they carved this stela and they carved it in hieroglyphs, because it was important; they carved it in demotic so that the people could read it; and they carved it in Greek so Ptolemy V could read it, because he couldn't read Egyptian. The Greeks never learned to read Egyptian when they were ruling. The only Greek whoever learned ancient Egyptian language was Cleopatra; we'll talk about that later.

So the Rosetta stone is basically a thank you letter from the priests of Egypt to Ptolemy V, saying thanks a lot, you're a good guy. Given that we now know what the Rosetta stone said, that it was a key to decipherment, I want to go to my last goal for this lecture, I want you to be able to read and write your own names in hieroglyphs. So to do that you're going to have to know how the language really works. Now, let me start by saying there are three ways a hieroglyph, a hieroglyphic symbol, can be used.

First, they can be used phonetically to represent a sound. For example, if you take the hieroglyph that looks like a hand, a hand hieroglyph, they are not talking about hands; that represents the sound *da*, a "D." If you look at the little rectangle hieroglyph, which, if you remember, was the first hieroglyph in King Ptolemy's name, that's a "P." Then you have the little semi-circle in Ptolemy's name, that's a "T." So those three symbols, the P, the T, and the D, those three, are alphabetic, just represent a sound. They're not talking about hands and rectangles and semi-circles.

Now, if we put those three hieroglyphs together, if we form them together, we have a word, DPT. The ancient Egyptians didn't write vowels; many ancient languages don't have vowels. For example, Hebrew did not write the vowels until very late. The reason is that most people are illiterate and these were just sort of *aide-memoirs* to help you remember things; it wasn't like the formal writing. So DPT, now we don't know how exactly it was pronounced, but let's say, call it "depet," we'll put "depet," we'll put in a little short "e" so it doesn't sound a little like Swedish or whatever. So we'll say "depet," that was a word. It's a phonetic word, three hieroglyphs used phonetically.

Now, the next use of a hieroglyph, there are three, remember. We're using it phonetically first. I can also, now by the way, the ancient Egyptian word "depet" meant boat; it was a word for boat. Now, I can also, if I want to clarify what the hand and the rectangle and the semi-circle mean, I could at that end of that word add a boat, a little picture of a boat; now that's helping me make clear what the meaning is. I'm using that hieroglyph like a picture of what it is. So the first three hieroglyphs—the "D," and the "P," and the "T," say boat, depet—and the next one helps clarify it. It determines the meaning for me; helps me determine the meaning. That use of a hieroglyph is called a determinative because it helps determine the meaning of a phonetic word. So that's the second way a hieroglyph can be used. After a bunch of phonetic sounds, giving you a picture of what it is. For example, if I wrote the word C-A-T, cat, and drew a little cat, the "C," and the "A," and the "T" are phonetic, and a little picture of the cat is helping me determine the meaning. So far we have two ways that hieroglyphs, hieroglyphic sounds, can be used either phonetically, or as a determinative, to give you a picture.

Now, what if I'm in a real hurry? I don't have time to write "D," the "P," the "T," draw a little boat; I want to get it done quickly. That's my third use of hieroglyphs. I can simply draw a picture of a boat and put a little line under it, a stroke, and that says it's a picture, that's all you're getting. That's called an ideogram. It's pictorial writing. This shows that I'm just doing it the fastest way I can; I'm giving you a picture. So three ways you can use a hieroglyph, three ways. You can use it either phonetically, represent a sound; as a determinative to help you determine the meaning of a phonetic word; or you can just use it like picture writing, like people always thought it was, just a simple drawing.

Now sometimes the ideograms are used—these ideograms are the picture writing—are used when space is limited. You know you're running out of space, it's sort of like the think it, the plan ahead sign, where the ahead runs off. If you're running out of space you start using these ideograms. Or, for example, on rings, if you wanted to put your name on a ring, which is a small surface, you might not have the room to spell out Montuhotep Herkepshef, or something like that, so you might want to try to do an ideogram of something, like the god Montu, a little picture or something like that. You do it in different ways. So, three different ways, determined often just sort of the circumstances.

Now, one thing I should tell you about Egyptian that I think is neat—it's the only language I know that can be written either from right to left, or left to right, or top to bottom. They can do it any way they wanted, and the reason is for artistic consideration. Think about a tomb. Let's say you're decorating a tomb and you have a doorway and you want to have a religious inscription over the doorway. You want it to say, "May I have all the bread and beer and things good and pure that the gods live on." Now you could write it either from left to right, or right to left, or if you wanted to be really artistic and have it really symmetrical, you could start at the middle of the door and write one inscription from right to left, reading outward from the middle. You could start the same inscription in the middle going the other way, and you've got this beautiful symmetrical double rendering of this prayer. And that's why they could write it from right to left or left to right, for artistic consideration. They were really into symmetry. You know Egypt is a very symmetrical land. You've got the Nile going down the middle; you've got the desert on both sides. They loved symmetry, they liked balance, and their language was done that way. Also, if you had a narrow space where you wanted to write something, you could write it from top to bottom.

Now, if you want to know, how do you read it, how do you know which way to read it, the answer is, you always read toward the mouths of the birds. So if you look at the birds, and if the mouth is like this, you read it this way, into the mouth, as if the bird is eating the direction it's going in. So you read always into the mouths of the birds and that's what always tells you which way to do it. It's never confusing. I know that sometimes it sounds like it might be, but it never is. It's an amazing language.

But, now, in my promise I said that you would all be able to read and write your names in hieroglyphs before this lecture is over. And here is how we're going to do it. At the end of your outlines is an appendix. I've got the entire Egyptian alphabet for you there. For example, the vulture, the bird is an "A," an "ah" sound. They didn't have full vowels; it's a semi-vowel. You'll see a foot; a foot is a "B" sound. You'll see our friend the hand; you'll see hand as "D." You'll see the "P," the rectangle. You'll see—all of that you'll see.

Now, what I want you to do is take that chart, and using that chart, figure out how your name would be written in hieroglyphs. First, you're going to be missing some letters, because some vowels aren't there. As I said, the Egyptians don't have—many vowels are missing. Just leave them out. And remember, what you're doing is, you're not translating your name. We don't call that translating; you're transliterating. Transliterating is taking the sound of your name—that's all you're going by, you don't care about the meaning of your name—that's translating. You're taking the sound of your name, and you're writing it in the Egyptian script. So, for example, if your name is Barbara, the first letter, you would look for a "B," and that's the foot. So the first letter in your name would be a "B." Now full vowel, but the vulture, the Egyptian vulture, the bird is an "ah" sound, that's close, so you'd put an "ah." So you would have a foot and a vulture. Then you have the mouth sound, the little oval, which is "R," "B-A-R," and repeat it again "B-A-R" because "Barbar." And at the end you would have another vulture. So, it would be foot, vulture, mouth, foot, vulture, mouth, vulture, would be Barbara. And you can all do that for all your names. I want you to try it. It will be fun. Try it out on friends, write friends' name. And your homework assignment is to write the names, transliterating them in hieroglyphs, of three famous people. And then show them to someone else with the chart and see if they can figure it out who the people you've written are. So that's your homework assignment, the only time I'll give you a homework assignment during the 48 lectures. But that one, I want you to try, and I think you'll find it a lot of fun.

So now you should know how the ancient Egyptian language worked, how the Rosetta stone helped decipher it, and I hope you can write your names in hieroglyphs. I'll see you next time.

Lecture Six
The First Nation in History

Scope:

Here we see Egypt become the first nation in history. We will also consider the first historical document in the world. From the time of the unification of Upper and Lower Egypt by King Narmer (Menes), it would take only a few hundred years to build a power that would dominate the Near East for thousands of years. We will show why the political structure of ancient Egypt made this possible and how the Narmer Palette tells this story.

Outline

I. Egypt was originally divided into separate kingdoms: Upper and Lower Egypt. By 3200 B.C., they appear to have been ruled by different kings.

   A. The crown was a symbol of royal power. In the south (Upper Egypt), it was white and conical in shape; in the north (Lower Egypt), it was red with a peak at the back.

   1. No crown has ever been found for the two kingdoms.

   2. The crowns were believed to have magical powers. It was the one thing that a pharaoh couldn't take with him to the next world.

   B. Communication between the two kingdoms was probably limited, making unification more of a labor. Travel, whether by donkey or boat, was difficult.

II. Egypt was united from the separate kingdoms into one nation about 3150 B.C., when King Narmer from the south conquered the north.

   A. The Narmer Palette, the world's first historical document (3150 B.C.), was discovered north of Aswan in 1897. A ceremonial palette made of slate, it was not intended for cosmetic use in daily life. It may have been used to grind cosmetics for offerings at a shrine to the gods.

   1. The Narmer Palette shows the beginning of writing, the first real hieroglyphs.

   2. Artistic conventions appear: The king was portrayed as the symbol of Egypt, and hierarchical proportions were used to distinguish kings from commoners.

3. The palette contains a complete story. Narmer, wearing the white crown and holding a mace in one hand, is about to smite his enemy, whom he is holding by the hair with the other hand. That enemy may have been the king of the north.

4. The enemy has a ring through his nose that is tied by a string to the falcon, symbol of the pharaoh.

5. "Registration" is recognizable on the palette—figures stand on defined planes or registers, rather than float haphazardly.

6. On the other side of the palette, we have the conclusion of the story. In the victory procession, we see the red crown on Narmer—representing the unification of Egypt—and the headless enemies vanquished by the new king.

7. Beneath Narmer are two fantastic beasts. Perhaps the intertwined necks of the beasts—panthers or leopards—are a symbol of the unification of Egypt.

8. Beneath them is a fortress being broken down by a bull, another symbol of Narmer.

B. The palette was probably carved by two different people, one doing each side. After all, the figures on each side are done in different styles. We may, in fact, have been reading the two sides in the wrong order, a mystery for future Egyptologists to ponder.

C. Why is the palette so important? For the story it tells. Now Egypt has a single king, a god on earth, Horus on earth. Other ancient nations had kings but not kings that were gods.

III. There are important benefits of a unified Egypt, as Narmer became the first king of the First Dynasty.

A. The all-powerful ruler, from Egypt to Plato's *Republic* to Thomas Hobbes's *Leviathan*, can do great things. (We give up our rights to a strong central government so that we will be safe.) Egypt, beginning with Narmer, could now rule the entire Mideast.

B. A standing army was possible, because centralization focuses resources where they are needed most.

C. The annual flooding of the Nile could now be turned to public advantage. Irrigation projects could be organized with large numbers of people working for the common good. Workers coaxed the Nile from its banks by irrigation ditches.

D. Egypt was the first nation in history with a powerful centralized government. The government would collapse at times, but the people would always go back to the "divine order" of a centralized government ruled by a pharaoh.

E. Such monuments as the pyramids were possible only because of a centralized government that facilitated the tradition of massive public works projects. The Egyptians used people, not beasts of burden, for large architectural undertakings.

F. It would take just a few hundred years after Narmer's conquest to begin the building of the great pyramids.

Essential Reading:

Michael Rice, *Egypt's Making*, Chapter 3.

Supplementary Reading:

Peter Clayton, *Chronicle of the Pharaohs*, pp. 14–19.

Questions to Consider:

1. What is the story told by the Narmer Palette?
2. What are the advantages of nationhood?

Lecture Six—Transcript
The First Nation in History

Hi. I've got a question for you: Did you do your homework? Did you write your name in hieroglyphs, and did you write the names of three other famous people in hieroglyphs? It's fun and you can practice it, keep it going. It's a skill that you'll lose if you don't use it, so keep trying to do it.

Now, remember in the first lecture I said that I was going to try to do this chronologically. I was trying to take things in order, but there would be some side trips. Well, the last two lectures have been the side trips. We've done Napoleon in Egypt and the discovery of the Rosetta stone, and then a little bit about how the Rosetta stone led to decipherment, and something about Egyptian language.

Well, I want to return to the chronological approach now. I want to go back to early Egypt. Now, remember we did prehistoric times, 700,000 years in 30 minutes. I want to come now to historic times, the very beginnings of writing in Egypt. And what we're going to discuss today is one document, the first historical document in the world, the Narmer palette. And we're going to use this document to see a few things about Egyptian civilization. One is we'll see the political setup with a king as the divine ruler of Egypt. And we'll also see why having such a political setup will enable Egypt to do great things.

But let me start with Egypt before it was a nation. Now, if you remember back to prehistory we left Egypt around 3200 B.C. A Nile Valley civilization populated by little villages, maybe 150 people here, 150 people here, perhaps 2,000 in all; we're not sure exactly of the numbers. And Egypt was divided into two kingdoms, Upper and Lower Egypt. And if you'll remember, Upper Egypt is beneath Lower Egypt because of the way the Nile flows. Well, right at the cusp of history in Egypt, written history, 3200 B.C. roughly, Upper Egypt seems to be ruled by a king and Lower Egypt by another king. And they had symbols, crowns. The kings had different crowns. It's interesting, isn't it, that somehow a hat becomes the symbol of authority, and it's remained that. The queen of England's policemen have special hats, everybody has special hats. And the kings of Egypt had special hats.

In the south it was the white crown, a tall white crown, kind of conical. In the north, it was a red crown, it's a shorter crown, has a little peak at the back, a little feather curling up in the front. So you have the tall white crown of the south and the red crown of the north.

I'll tell you something really interesting about the crowns, and this is my theory. It certainly may be wrong, so you shouldn't take it as fact. The fact is that no crown has ever been found. We do not have the crown of any king of Egypt. For 3,000 years the pharaohs wore the red and the white crown; none has ever been found. Tutankhamen's tomb was discovered intact. Everything he packed in there for the next world was there—no crown, no crown. My theory—and this is the part that really may be wrong, I'll just present it—is that I don't think there was more than one crown in existence at any one time. I think it was like—it was a magical thing—the crowns were believed to have actual magical powers, and I think it was the one thing that when a pharaoh died he couldn't take with him to the next world. His successor got the crown. So I think there was probably only one red crown and one white crown in existence at any one time. And that's why it wasn't found in Tutankhamen's tomb. But that's just a theory. But the important thing is that very early on in Egyptian history, these crowns were the symbol of power.

Now, there was probably some communication between Upper and Lower Egypt, but it was limited. Travel wasn't easy, remember, in ancient Egypt. You had the Nile. That was a good way to go long distance, but the common man certainly couldn't afford a boat. And the only other way you went anyplace in Egypt was by donkey. It was the donkey for the short haul and boats for the long haul. So communication was probably limited.

But then around the best guess is 3150 B.C., Upper Egypt and Lower Egypt are unified. It becomes one country. And how is it unified? Apparently, by a king from the south conquering in the north, and that king's name is Narmer. And we have an object called the Narmer palette, which is what I call the first historical document in the world. It tells of the unification of Egypt. And what I want to do today is tell you about the Narmer palette and how it tells the story of the unification of Egypt.

Now, first about the palette itself. It's a palette that's about two feet high and it's made of slate, but isn't an ordinary slate palette. Now, as you remember, the ordinary Egyptians used palettes for grinding their cosmetics. They would take a little bit, for example, of carbon, charcoal from a fire, mix it with fat, and grind it on the palette, and that became eye makeup; it's the first cosmetics in the world. And they would put it onto their eyes. And also, in desert countries it helps absorbs the glare; it's not just decorative. That's why when you look at football players they are wearing basically eye makeup under their eyes, black, to absorb the glare so it doesn't go into your eye.

So this was not one of those palettes though; this is a highly decorated carved palette. It's what we call a ceremonial palette. It was probably never used in a house; it's too big, it's too fancy, it's too elaborate. It was probably a temple object. It may have even been used to grind the cosmetics for a statue of the god. See, every temple, in the back of the temple had an area called the holy of holies, a shrine where only the priests could go. And in that holy of holies was a bronze statue of the god, whoever was the god of that temple. So if it was Amun, there would be a statute of Amun. And the priests every morning would throw open the doors and anoint the statue with oils, cosmetics, give it an offering of foods, and close the doors. This may have been a palette that was used to anoint the gods. It's really big, beautiful, and important. But it tells a story, and that's why I say it's the first historical document in the world.

Now, the palette does a few things for us. First, it's the beginning of language. This is where we get our first real hieroglyphs telling a story. Another thing is it sets a kind of artistic invention, artistic style that is going to last for 3,000 years. This is where we're going to see the king as a symbol of Egypt. The king is really the way you see Egypt; he was the icon. Egypt meant the pharaoh; he was that central. The pharaoh's role was to keep divine order in the world. The Egyptians had this strong concept of divine order, that there was a certain order and Egypt was on top of that order. And the king's job was to make the right offerings to the gods; make sure that the gods were pleased and divine order would stay. So the king is the symbol of Egypt.

Now, in addition, not only is he a symbol of Egypt, he's presented in what we call hierarchal proportion. The king is bigger than everybody. When you look on a temple wall, everybody is not the same size. The king is about four or five times the size of a commoner, and he is almost the same size as the gods, because he is a god on earth. He is the god Horus on earth. So, on this Narmer palette we see a king who is larger than everybody else, and he is the symbol of Egypt.

Now, let me tell you what is on this palette. On one side of the palette—and it's carved on both sides—on one side of the palette, we see a king. He's got this tall white crown, so we know he is from the south, he is wearing the white crown. And he is in a pose that will be repeated for 3,000 years of Egyptian history. It's called smiting; he's about to kill his enemy. He has his arm raised and in his hand he's got a mace. Now, a mace is a weapon; it's basically a rock on a stick. It's a stick that can be held in the hand with a big rock on the end of it, and you smash your enemy's skull with it. And Narmer is about to smite; he's got his hand raised. And in his other hand he is holding an enemy. It's a man with a beard, and he's got him by the hair. This is a traditional pose that you're going to see for 3,000 years. Ramses the Great, thousands of years later, is going to show the same thing; he's got the enemies by the hair and he is about to smite theim with a mace. So Narmer is a king from the south about to smite the enemy.

Now, who is this enemy? Well, there are some hieroglyphs in the background that give you a clue. Behind the enemy we see swampy plants. We see a kind of marsh, and we see some plants coming out. That might suggest this enemy is the ruler of the Delta area. Now the Delta, of course, is a marshy swampy area in the north of Egypt. And you know why it's called the Delta? That's because of the Greeks. When the Greeks came into Egypt, the swampy marshy area was a triangle, shaped like the Greek letter *delta*, so they called it a delta. It didn't have anything to do with swamp or marsh; it was just triangular, and now we've picked that up. So this person who was about to be killed by Narmer is perhaps the ruler of the Delta. And when you look at the palette there are some brutal things there. One of the things is, the enemy, this poor guy from the Delta who was about to be killed by Narmer has a ring placed through his nose and the ring is attached to a string, which is held by a falcon. Now the falcon is the symbol of a pharaoh. So the pharaoh has the enemy through the nose. This poor guy is about to be dispatched by the king of Egypt.

Now, quite interesting, behind the king is some little tiny guy. He's about one-fifth the size of Narmer. And you have to look really close when you're looking at the Narmer palette, which is in the Egyptian

Museum in Cairo, you have to look very close, but he's carrying sandals. Carrying a pair of sandals. He is the sandal bearer to the king, carries the king's sandals. Now, I don't think that the king really wanted to change his shoes very often. But this is an official title; he is an important official. He is not just a "roadie" who is bringing stuff, a gofer. No, this guy is like maybe the viceroy of Egypt, and he is behind the king. But he's only about one-fifth the size.

Now how do we know this is Narmer; how do we know his name? At the top, very top of the palette is a rectangle. Now, that rectangle is called in Egyptian a *serekh*; it's a rectangle that represents the palace. This is where the king lived. And inside that little rectangle are two hieroglyphs—a chisel and a fish. Those are the hieroglyphs for Nar and Mer—"chisel" is "Mer," "fish" is "Nar," and that's how we know his name. Who's in the palace? Who's in the rectangle? Narmer. This is the first name we have of a king of Egypt. Narmer is almost certainly the first king of Egypt, and he writes his name in his palace facade or *serekh*.

So, we've got Narmer, the beginnings of hieroglyphs, and we've got him smiting the enemy from the Delta. And if you look at the bottom of the palette, that side, you'll see enemies who kind of almost look like they're swimming. They have probably been killed, maybe, or they are trying to flee, something like that. They look just like the guy who has got this nose ring through him, this poor guy. But Narmer is about to conquer these guys.

Now, an important thing to notice also on the palette, if you stare at it in the Egyptian Museum in Cairo, is that the palette has everybody standing on registers; there is like a line beneath the feet. This is another artistic tradition. You don't just let them float around; it's kind of too confusing. They would look a little disjointed. So registration, as we call it, having the people always stand on something, is a tradition. Even if you look at hieroglyphs, whenever you look at hieroglyphs in ancient Egypt, the birds are always standing on something; they are not just kind of floating around. So this is only one side of the palette, only one side, but it's telling a big story.

If you look very closely at Narmer, you'll see something really neat. He's wearing a belt. He's got a kind of girdle around him, and that's some sort of official garment. He's wearing some official garment.

And if you look very closely at the little figure, this guy is kind of hunched over and he's holding his shoulder. Now why is he holding his shoulder? He's wearing a garment that doesn't fit him. He's wearing a leopard skin. The leopard skin is the sign of a high priest. So, he's also the vizier of Egypt probably and a high priest. And for another 3,000 years, this leopard skin is going to be the sign of the high priest. So think about it, a leopard skin is not a form-fitting garment. He's got to hold it, he's hunched over, it's not very comfortable, but this is something that's going to be a tradition.

And there is one other thing if you look at this little guy, he's got a little necklace on and what that necklace is is probably his seal of authority. It's a cylinder seal that was rolled out in clay to stamp his name when he had to do official things for the king. So we've got Narmer, and he's already got an official behind him and he is conquering this Delta, this poor Delta, guy. But that's only one side of the palette.

On the other side, we have the conclusion of the story. We've got what happens. Now, what we have at the end, on the other side, is King Narmer, but he's not wearing the white crown anymore. He's wearing the red crown, the short red crown. He has conquered the north and now is the king of Upper and Lower Egypt. It's the unification of Egypt. And from Narmer on, the pharaoh will wear what we call the double crown. He will wear a crown that is a composite of both the red and the white. It will be the tall white, and in front of it will be the short red one. That is the sign that he is the king of both Upper and Lower Egypt. So Narmer is the first uniter of Egypt, and Egypt becomes the first nation in history. That is a first.

But that's not all the palette tells us. If you look beneath or near Narmer, there is a procession going on. There are little people, and they are holding poles, and on top of the poles are little symbols of the areas where they come from. They are marching in procession, and they are marching toward people who are lying down, have their hands tied behind their backs, and their heads have been cut off. These are the vanquished; Narmer has won and he's cut off the heads of the enemies. And we've got our little vizier, the little guy following behind.

Now, beneath Narmer, though, are two fantastic animals. They don't exist in real life. They look kind of like panthers or leopards with very long legs, very long necks, like a giraffe. And the necks are intertwined. They are somehow uniting these two panthers, and I think that may be the symbol of the unification of Egypt; the intertwined necks are Upper and Lower Egypt being joined together. And beneath them is a fortress, a walled city of some sort, big crenulations on the top, you know, the bumps that archers like stay behind, and that wall is being broken down by a bull. The bull will also become a symbol of Narmer. Narmer has come to the Delta, a fortified city, broken down the walls, killed the king of the north, taken the enemies, and he is now in control. So Narmer becomes the first pharaoh of the first dynasty. He is sometimes also called Menes, by the way. The general theory is that Narmer and Menes—there are different kings lists—are the same. They are each the first king of the first dynasty.

Now, why is the Narmer palette so important? Let me tell you one curious thing about it, that is, again, my personal theory and it's kind of strange, but I think it might be right. If you look very closely, very closely, at the hieroglyphs and the images that are drawn on the Narmer palette—and I spent hours standing in the Egyptian Museum looking at it, I've looked at large photos of it—I think you will also be convinced, as I am, that the Narmer palette was carved by two different people. One side is carved by one person, and one side is carved by the other.

Now, why do I say that? If you look, for example, at the *serekh*, those rectangles that represent the palace, you'll see they have different numbers of doors in them, they are totally different. The same artist would never do that. And the same is true for other elements of the palette. If you look at the figures, they are carved completely differently. Now, I don't know what it means, I'm not sure. But I'll give you just one suggestion that, again, is theory, and I emphasize this theory, but it kind of shakes the established interpretation of the Narmer palette. What I wonder is this: If the palette is indeed carved by two different people, and I'm quite sure it is, why? It's a small object. Why did two different people do it? Now, it could be something trivial. It could indeed be, say, the artist was sick, he said, "Harry you take over." Somebody else did it. Could be. But it also could be that some time passed between the carving of the first side and the carving of the second side, and that could mean that we may be reading the palette wrong. How do we know to read the side that I said is the first side first? Maybe we should read it the other way and we get a different story. It's just a possibility.

I suggest it for another reason; I have another reason why I think we might be reading it backward. Which side would you consider the first side, the most important? I would consider the one that has the round oppression of the intertwined necks, because that's where you would grind your cosmetics. That's where the cosmetics were ground, and certainly that would be the first side, the most important. So there is just a slight chance that this first historical document in the world may be being read backward, but I just throw that out as a suggestion. It's a kind of partly-baked idea, but I just wanted to mention that at least you know that the Narmer palette was carved by two different people, and that I think everybody would agree with.

Now, why is this so important? Well, it's not just that it's the first document in history. It's that it's going to set up Egypt in such a way that Egypt can rule the entire Near East, because now Egypt has a single king who is a god on earth. Remember, that poor little guy from the Delta with a ring in his nose is being held by a falcon. The pharaoh was Horus on earth. Remember, Horus was the son of Osiris, who was killed, he's the avenger; he's the one who set it right, who killed—who defeats his evil uncle Seth. So the pharaoh as Horus is a god on earth. Now, other nations in the Middle East, ancient nations, had kings, but the king was not a god. Only Egypt had a god, and there are real virtues to this.

So we have Egypt unified under a god-king. Now, why is that great? I'll tell you why. If you have a completely powerful ruler you can do almost anything. You know, Plato said it. Plato wrote a book called *The Republic*, and in *The Republic* Plato talks about what is the ideal form of government. What's the best way to rule a nation? And Plato came up with, "You should have a philosopher king ruling." He was a philosopher, of course, so he would want a philosopher ruling. But there was a rationale behind it. Plato said, "You want a philosopher, because you want a society that's just, that's fair." And justice—who better to determine that than a philosopher? But you want him also to be a king, because you want him to have absolute power. You don't want him to get stuck in bureaucratic red tape. You want him to know what's right and then do it—no ifs, ands, or buts. So Plato said the best government is a philosopher king.

Thomas Hobbes, the political philosopher, said much later that the ideal form of government is a monarch, a king. And he, of course, was English under a king. But the idea was that without a ruler with real absolute power, we'd live in a state of jungle; we'd be killing each other. So what we do, he said is that we give up our rights so that we're safe. We have a monarch who will rule us and tell us what to do. So this notion that the best government is an absolute ruler may really come out of Egypt.

Now, with a king who was a god, the absolute ruler, you can do great things. And let me tell you about what Egypt could do because they had a Narmer, somebody unifying Egypt, and they would have it for 3,000 years. First, you can build a standing army. You can say, "We need an army. You, you, you, let's go," and that's it. You've got a god-king, you don't discuss it. With a standing army you can march out, conquer other lands. And by the way, there is a pottery fragment with Narmer's name on it all the way in the Sinai, near Palestine actually. That may mean that Narmer took the army outside of Egypt, who knows. It's just a fragment; it doesn't mean that much. But it suggests we've got kind of an expansionist viewpoint now—you can have an army.

But more important than an army, much more important, you can marshal the resources of a country by fear; you say it and it's done. And you can get great things done, and let me say exactly what I mean by that—irrigation ditches. Now, if you remember, Herodotus, our Greek tourist, said that Egypt is the gift of the Nile. What he meant was that the rich top soil is deposited during innundation. Now, let me describe innundation for you as the Egyptians saw it. First understand that innundation, when the Nile rose and overflowed its banks, was not viewed as a natural phenomenon. The Egyptians did not know the source of the Nile. As a matter of fact, we didn't know the source of the Nile until the middle of the 19th century; that's why you had guys like Burton and Speke exploring, and Bruce, going in search of the source of the Nile.

Now, the main cause of innundation is the monsoon season in Ethiopia. The waters torrent down, pour into the Nile, and as the Nile flows northward you get two Niles joining at Khartoum, the white and the blue Nile. Now, think about what the Egyptians saw during innundation. First, the Nile turned red. Now, it turned red because it was carrying with it the top soil, the rich red soil, from Ethiopia northward. So first it turns red; then it turns green, that's the slower moving vegetation coming from the south. The top soil moves quickly, it's small, it's suspended in the water. The vegetation is floating on top, turns green, then it rises 30 feet. It must have been a magical event, and it happened every year around July, like clockwork, remarkable. They didn't know the source. They thought it was the gods around the area of Aswan in the south of Egypt opening doors and caverns underneath the Nile that caused it to overflow the banks. But now, as it deposits the rich top soil, this enables Egypt to grow the crops.

But how can you increase the yield; how can you really make it sort of maximum? This is where Narmer, this is where a strong king, comes in. He can marshal the entire forces of Egypt for work projects that are to the benefit of all the Egyptians. And you know what that is—irrigation ditches. What Egypt learned to do was to coax the Nile inward to give you as much top soil as possible inward and to keep the Nile waters inward. So they dug irrigation ditches. This was a major work project that involved all the farmers. Now remember, of course, farmers—farming and farmers is what Egypt was about, it was an agrarian society, 90 percent were farmers—so you take all the farmers, and you say, it's time to get ready, the innundation is coming. The priest astronomers knew when it was coming. And you start digging the irrigation ditches. So that when the floods come and it overflows the banks, it will bring the water inland and you have fields and fields to irrigate. That's what you can do if you have a powerful centralized government. So, Egypt is the first nation in history with a powerful centralized government. You know, Egypt will have times when the government collapses, when horrible things happen; we call them intermediate periods. We don't even know—they're dark ages. But they will always go back to a pharaoh, a god-king, as the ruler, because that was the government they knew that worked. That's what they thought was part of divine order. Divine order involved centralized government with a pharaoh telling everyone what to do. That's partly why the Narmer palette is so important.

Now, one other thing. If you can get people together for working for the public good, what else can you do besides irrigation ditches? Now the answer is, build pyramids. You see the skills; there is a reason why it's Egypt that builds pyramids and not the other countries. You had a strong centralized government with a tradition of marshaling manpower, and, remember, the Egyptians did not use beasts of burden very well. When you hauled big blocks of stone, it was with people, not animals. The only time they really used animals, beasts of burden, was for plowing; that's the first use of domesticated animals. But when it came to big blocks, moving stones, we have pictures of them moving huge statues and it's lots of guys pulling on ropes who are doing it. So, if you don't have beasts of burden it's manpower that you need, and a strong centralized government is going to do it for you. You can say, okay, we're going to do this.

So, I think that what made Egypt capable of building pyramids is really two things. One is they had this strong centralized government with a king, with a head, but they also had this tradition of public work projects where they were told to do things for the good, for the benefit of all. And once they could do that it was a short hop to the building of the pyramids of Egypt. It would take just a few hundred years from Narmer's conquest of ancient Egypt, from unifying it, coming from the south, defeating the king of the north, and wearing the double crown, in a few hundred years, Egypt would be building the Great Pyramid of Egypt. But that's a story for next time.

Lecture Seven
The Rise of the Old Kingdom

Scope:

We will see the development of Egypt into a great nation led by a single all-powerful ruler, the king. Here traditions are set that will last for thousands of years: a capital city, separate burial places for the kings, solar boats to make the journey to the next world. It is also the time when the pattern for pharaohs' behavior is established for future dynasties. We will also see how the transition was made from simple burials to the first pyramid in history.

Outline

I. A capital will be established at Memphis in the north, and it all began with Narmer. Dynasty I (3035–2890 B.C.) included the earliest kings.

   A. Excavations at Abydos, in the south, revealed the tombs of the early kings.

   B. Hor-Aha founded Memphis, in the north, as a capital city. (*Egypt* actually derives from the local name for Memphis.) The location was crucial for strategic reasons: to guard against invasion from the sea, because invasion across the desert was too difficult.

   C. The kings of Dynasty I were buried at Abydos, the sacred city where Osiris was buried in the famous myth.

      1. These are simple underground mud-brick tombs of King Djer, Den, and others, which have been robbed.

      2. Archeologist Flinders Petrie excavated these tombs in the late nineteenth century. To avoid looting, he paid his workers market value for their discoveries. (Other excavators tried to confiscate everything.) At one point, they found a detached mummy's arm in King Djer's tomb, wearing the oldest royal jewelry ever discovered. Petrie weighed it and paid for it in gold sovereigns. A curator in Cairo later threw away the arm and kept only the jewelry!

3. Burials for kings were also at Saqqara, named for Sokar, god of the dead. Why two burials? One burial site was a false one, or cenotaph. Thus, the two represented a symbolic way of denoting power over the north and south. We're not sure, for certain pharaohs, which burial was the real one.

II. Dynasty II (2890–2686 B.C.) was a period as long as the history of the United States, but little is known of it. It was the succeeding dynasty, however, that established Egypt as a civilization of renown.

III. Dynasty III (2686–2613 B.C.) was a time of greatness.

A. Zoser (2686–2649 B.C.) was the first pyramid builder. He elaborated on the older burial practices of Egypt.

1. Sand-pit burials, originally used for the dead, were impermanent by nature, uncovered by wind and jackals in search of decomposing flesh. The Egyptians began removing sand to ground level and cutting into the rock to carve a tomb.

2. They would erect a *mastaba*, or rectangular shelter, above the tomb. Imhotep, Zoser's architect, decided to stack mastaba on mastaba, creating a step effect; from the mastaba, the pyramid developed.

3. The Step Pyramid of Saqqara, grand in size and conception, was the first stone building in history, probably three or four times larger than any other building on the planet.

4. Next to the pyramid is a little room where Zoser included a small statue of himself. In case his body was destroyed, his soul could live there until he was resurrected.

5. He also built chapels at the pyramid. The pyramid imitates reed construction techniques, only using stone.

6. Here Zoser planned a complex intended for use as a courtyard for the *heb-sed* and other rituals. The *heb-sed* festival celebrated the rejuvenation of the aging pharaoh every thirty years.

7. The tomb of Imhotep, the architect, is still missing. Zoser permitted him to be buried near his own tomb. Professor Walter B. Emery, close on the scent of finding it, died before it was discovered.

8. Zoser also had a southern burial, just a couple of hundred yards away from the Step Pyramid. Tiles on the inside, made of the ceramic called *faience*, show him running a *heb-sed* festival.

B. Horus Sekhemkhet, Zoser's successor, ruled from 2649–2643 B.C.

1. Sekhemkhet was going to build a Step Pyramid like Zoser's, but it was only a few meters high when he died. Its stone walls are still rough, so we know the blocks were not finished by workers until they were on site. The intact pyramid was discovered in 1951.

2. The burial chamber was still sealed. Though a great discovery was expected, Sekhemkhet's stone sarcophagus turned out to be empty. Gold jewelry was found on the floor of the tomb but no body.

3. Perhaps Sekhemkhet was buried in a second tomb, and the empty one was only a decoy for grave robbers. Unfortunately, the tomb robbers were usually the ones who built the tombs! We still haven't found the real tomb of Sekhemkhet.

C. Egypt's rise to greatness will continue.

Essential Reading:

Aidan Dodson, *Monarchs of the Nile*, Chapters IV and V.

Supplementary Reading:

Peter Clayton, *Chronicle of the Pharaohs*, pp. 32–60.

Questions to Consider:

1. What traditions were established during this early period?

2. How did pyramid building evolve from earlier buildings?

Lecture Seven—Transcript
The Rise of the Old Kingdom

Hello again. What I'd like to do is start by reviewing a little bit what we talked about last time because that leads directly into what I'm going to discuss today. Remember we talked about Narmer and how Narmer was the first king of Egypt and united Egypt. Upper and Lower Egypt became one large nation, the first nation in history. Well, what I'd like to do today is show you the fruits of that, to show you just what you can do if you have a nation under one strong ruler. We're going to see the rise of the Old Kingdom. We're going to see Egypt really become great, and it's all going to happen because they had a king.

Now, what we're going to see is first a capital, a city where the bureaucracy takes place, is established, and that's a sign of a nation. Villages up and down the Nile aren't a nation, but if you have a united group of people they need a central place, and we will see a capital established at Memphis in the north of Egypt. We'll also see traditions that will last 3,000 years. We'll see behavior patterns laid down for the pharaoh that future pharaohs will follow centuries later, and it all starts with Narmer, the first king of the First Dynasty.

Let me say some things about these kings of the First Dynasty. Up until the nineteenth century they were practically legendary. We didn't know anything about them. We had a couple of names but no monuments, no evidence that they really existed. As far as we knew, they could have been mythological. Then excavations at a city in the south, Abydos, revealed that they had tombs. These are kings with names like Aha, Den, Djer—early kings. We know something about Aha. He founded the first capital city at Memphis. As a matter of fact, the word "Egypt" comes from Memphis. Originally Memphis was called Hikuptah. It was the place of the god Ptah. When the Greeks came in, the first big city they hit was Memphis. They said, "What's the name of this place?" "Heqaptah." It became *Aegyptos*, which became "Egypt." So Egypt really comes out of Memphis, the first capital.

The reason they established the capital at Memphis was for strategic reasons. It's in the north; it's about maybe 15 miles from Cairo, from modern Cairo, and Egypt was only worried about invasion from the sea. Egypt was really quite protected. If you think about the geography, it's got desert on either side—not easy to cross. To cross a desert it would take a kind of organizational skill that no other nation had to get across a desert. You need water stations. You need supplies. So they weren't worried about their eastern and western borders yet. But maybe an invasion could come by the water, by the peoples on the other side of Mediterranean. So if you establish your capital at Memphis you've got a bit of a buffer, you can hear them coming, and then you can repulse them. So Memphis becomes the capital.

But these first kings of the First Dynasty aren't buried at Memphis; they are buried far away. They are buried at Abydos, this southern city. Now, why Abydos? The answer is, if you remember the myth of Isis and Osiris, where Osiris was hacked to pieces and then reassembled by Isis, his wife, well, according to the myth those pieces were put back together and buried at Abydos. So Abydos becomes the burial place of Osiris. It's the sacred city. Everybody— everybody wanted to be associated with Osiris. They wanted to resurrect just like Osiris. If you could have a burial place near him, perhaps you, too, would resurrect. So the kings of the First Dynasty are buried at Abydos—they have burials at Abydos.

Now, let me describe these burials. They are not fancy affairs yet. Egypt hasn't learned how to do it really big-time yet. They are basically pits in the sand. They are large. They are lined with mud bricks so the sand doesn't come in and fill it in immediately—they are mud brick pits. And in it the pharaohs were placed along with grave goods, undoubtedly.

They've all been robbed—all of them were robbed. These burials were excavated in the late nineteenth century by Sir Flinders Petrie. Now, remember, Petrie was the one who figured out that pots can tell you what comes earlier and what comes later, and Petrie excavated the sites that nobody wanted because, as I said before, he wasn't looking for treasure, he was looking for knowledge. Well, Petrie excavated here, and he discovered the earliest burials of Egypt, the kings' earliest burials. These little burials had in front of them a stela: the large stone, round-topped. On that stela was a *serekh*. Remember the palace facade—that rectangle. Inside it would be the king's name, but standing on top of that stela was a falcon. The Pharaoh was associated with Horus. This is the first name of the king, the Horus name. These mastabas yielded a few treasures, though. Petrie knew what he was doing.

Let me tell you about the excavation techniques in those days. Petrie did something that no one else ever did: He paid his excavators for what they found. Every other excavator in Egypt simply thought it was their right—they are paying the workmen, the diggers—and they expected the diggers to bring everything that they found, but it didn't happen that way. It was often said in the nineteenth century of certain excavators that they only found large statues, never small objects. What that meant was the workmen were stealing the small objects to sell on the antiquities market. Petrie wanted to do away with this. So what Petrie did was, when anybody found a small object, perhaps gold, perhaps just a beautiful bracelet, he would look at the object and pay the workmen the fair market value. So he knew that he got all of the small objects on his digs.

Well, it paid off for Petrie at Abydos. He was away from the tomb while the workmen were excavating. It was the tomb of the king Djer, and the workmen came to him and said, "We found a mummy's arm and on it is a gold bracelet." Petrie's workmen had been trained not to move things. The arm was in a wall; it was somehow stuck in a wall. Probably what happened was robbers came and robbed the tomb. One robber finds this mummy, the arm, the arm with bracelets on it; doesn't want his fellow robbers to see that he got something good; hides it in a wall; and then leaves but never returns to get it for some reason. So the workmen came and said, "Professor Petrie, we've got a mummy's arm with gold bracelets on it."

So Petrie had the arm brought to him. It had two bracelets. One was a gold bracelet with *serekhs*, those rectangles that represent the king, the palace, and on top of them falcons, little gold falcons. This was a king's bracelet. This is the oldest royal jewelry we have, on the arm of Djer. Now I'll tell you what Petrie did. Petrie looked at it, and to establish the value he took the gold bracelet and weighed it against English gold sovereigns, and he gave the workmen the gold sovereigns. So he gave them the gold value, they were very happy, and Petrie had the oldest royal jewelry, which might otherwise have been stolen.

I'll tell you what happened to the bracelet afterwards and the mummy's arm. The mummy's arm, which is the oldest relic of a pharaoh we have, was sent to the Egyptian Museum in Cairo. This is in the 1890s, late nineteenth century. The curator Brugsch of the Egyptian Museum in Cairo looked at the jewelry, was very impressed, took off the jewelry, and threw away the arm. The oldest royal body or part of a body that we have was thrown away. Petrie, in his later memoirs, said a wonderful thing when he was recounting this incident. When he talks about the curator throwing away the arm of King Djer, he says, "Sometimes a museum is a dangerous place." That's what happened to King Djer. But these burials at Abydos are important because they established that these kings that we knew only in name before are real people. They lived; they walked the earth.

Now, there is a bit of a mystery about these burials, and it's still disputed. There are two burials for these kings. There is a burial also in the north for these pharaohs. They have another burial at Saqqara. The name Saqqara comes from the god's name Sokar, who is the god of the dead, one of the gods of the dead. "Sokar" became "Saqqara," "the place of Sokar." Saqqara was used as an Old Kingdom burial site in the early part of Egyptian history for a long time.

Why did these kings have tombs both at Saqqara and Abydos? Well, one is a false burial, what we call a cenotaph. The reason to have two burials is that the pharaoh is really showing he is king of Upper and Lower Egypt, of the north and of the south, so he will have burials in both places. What's debated today is we're not 100 percent sure for which pharaoh which was the real burial. Was it at Saqqara, or was it at Abydos? We're not sure. But they had two burials, and this will be a practice for pharaohs later on, as you'll see.

So this is the First Dynasty. The Second Dynasty lasts for 200 years, as long as America has been in business, but we know hardly anything about it, just a few names. That gives you an idea of how remote this is in time for us. The Third Dynasty, the one that comes next, is where it all happens. It's where Egypt becomes great and powerful and does great things, and it starts with King Zoser, the builder of the first pyramid.

Now, let me give you a little bit of tomb archaeology, a little bit of the history of the development of architecture. Remember from the lesson on prehistoric Egypt that they buried originally in sandpit burials, just simple burials. What happened frequently is that the sand would blow away, exposing the body. Animals would get at it, usually jackals, by the way. There is an interesting thing about the jackal and why jackals are associated with funerals and funerary rites. The jackal has an unusual digestive system. It prefers decayed meat, so it prowls cemeteries. That's why jackals are associated in ancient Egypt with the dead. Often jackals would get at these bodies from the sandpit burials, eat it, and destroy it, and it became very clear that a sandpit burial was not permanent, that something better had to be done.

Well, what did they do? They removed the sand down to bedrock when they were doing a burial. They would cut in the rock a pit, and that's where they would bury and cover it over with stone, and then you had a permanent burial. Eventually these rock-cut burials in the ground became elaborate, fancy. Someone got the idea early on that you could put a superstructure over it, a kind of rectangular enclosure made of mud bricks at first, and you could even have a room in it where somebody could go in and pay their respects to the dead. This kind of burial, this rectangular, above-ground burial, is called in Arabic a *mastaba*. It's the Arabic word for "bench," because it's rectangular like a bench. So these mastabas are the early burials, and the pharaohs in Saqqara have mastabas.

From the mastaba it's just a short jump to the pyramid, and let me explain why. The king who really is given credit for starting with the first pyramid is King Zoser, Third Dynasty, and we know the name of his architect, who probably really is the one who should get the credit, Imhotep. The reason we know his name is a statue base, just a base of a statue, a couple of feet—you just see the feet, it's broken off—but there is an inscription around the base, and it talks about Imhotep, and it gives his titles. Imhotep was the royal architect of Zoser. So he is probably the one who had the idea for the first pyramid in history.

What he did was this: He was just building a big mastaba for Zoser. That's all he was doing. They were planning a mastaba, a large one, big as a football field. Then he had the idea, let's make it special. Let's put another mastaba on top of it. So you would have a mastaba with a second mastaba, a little smaller, though, so you have like a step effect. Then they decided to make it even bigger, so they enlarged the base and made another mastaba on top of that one. He had three mastabas, and they kept going until you get five layers on top, the Step Pyramid of Saqqara. It is the first pyramid that we have.

It's not a true pyramid—that's why we call it the Step Pyramid—but there are some remarkable features about this pyramid.

First, what I find most amazing, it's the first building in stone in the history of the world. To me, it would seem as if you would start with small things. You would have lots of small buildings around and learn how to work stone. Then you go to something bigger, and you would see transitions. But, no, this is the first building in stone in the history of the world, and it's grand. It was probably three or four times taller than any other building on the planet. It must have been incredible to watch it being built. If you were a kid in Saqqara watching the pharaoh's tomb being built, it must have been amazing.

It wasn't just the pyramid that he built, though. There is an entire complex that goes with it. Zoser also had next to his pyramid a little room which is called a *serdab*. It's a technical architectural term in Egypt. A *serdab* is a little room where he included a statue of himself, life-size, and the *serdab* is neat. It's like a telephone booth, practically, that size, made out of stone. It has two holes drilled in it so Zoser's statue can look out for eternity. This statue has a purpose. In case Zoser's body was destroyed for some reason, perhaps by tomb robbers, perhaps by the elements, water table, whatever—if his body were destroyed, this statue would be where his soul would know it could live until it resurrected. So it would take the place of Zoser's mummy.

In addition to this *serdab*, as we call it, Zoser also built chapels in stone, all around the pyramid complex, all these little chapels. These were for religious ceremonies, for eternity, though. Remember, this is the first building in stone. Nothing like it has ever been done. And let me say this about the architecture: They didn't know how to build in stone, really. They were doing amazing things. For example, they were imitating what they were used to building in wood and in straw and in papyrus. They were imitating it in stone. So, for example, where they had wooden doors that would swing open, well, they would build a door out of stone that looked like a wooden door, but it couldn't swing. It was too heavy, too big. It was just decorative; it was a false door. But they were just imitating what they were used to building.

Even the columns in the complex—there is a hall where you enter the complex that has columns, but those columns, if you look at them carefully, they look like they are fluted. They have lines going down them. What they imitate are bundles of papyrus tied together. That's how they built columns before stone buildings, simply long stalks looking like sugar canes bundled together, and that was a pillar, so they built it out of stone. Everything looks like it's made out of wood, made out of papyrus, but it's just imitated in stone.

In addition, Zoser was going to celebrate a festival for eternity. It's called the Heb-sed Festival. It's one of those things that we've been puzzling about in Egyptology for many years, how it started. Let me give you a kind of tradition. The pharaoh was the physical ruler of Egypt. He wasn't just like the queen of England, a figurehead, a political ruler. He was literally the one who had to ride out in battle. He was the one who had to lead the army. He was the one who had to do it all. What happens if the pharaoh becomes old and feeble? What do you do? Well, there is a tradition, people talk about it, that in the very early days the pharaoh was killed ritually—literally but ritually—when he got too old so that a new king could take his place. We don't have a lot of evidence for that, but we talk about it.

But then came a ritual that we know for sure that happened. At some point a pharaoh would say, "Well, I might be getting old, but I can have a religious ceremony which will magically rejuvenate me." This is called the *heb-sed* festival. It's a festival in which the pharaoh would run a racecourse, a short one, I'm sure. He would wrestle with younger men. He would shoot arrows to show that he was still accurate, he could still see things well. And after that festival he would be rejuvenated by magic. He would be young again. It was much better than being killed. This festival was celebrated every 30 years. So, after a Pharaoh had ruled for 30 years, he would celebrate his *heb-sed* festival. Zoser built a *heb-sed* courtyard. It was an area where he would celebrate his festival for eternity so that, when he got to the next world, every 30 years he could continue to be rejuvenated.

The Step Pyramid is an amazing, amazing monument, and it's probably due to the architect Imhotep. The search for Imhotep's tomb is one of the great stories of all time. Walter B. Emery, an Egyptologist in the 1950s, decided to look for Imhotep's tomb, and he had an idea. Zoser was buried at Saqqara. Probably as a thank you to his architect, Zoser would permit Imhotep to be buried near him. So it was believed that the tomb of Imhotep was at Saqqara, but where? Well, Imhotep had a tremendous reputation. He was not only an architect, he was a physician, and he later became deified as a god. Even the Greek god Asclepius is really related to Imhotep. The Greek god of healing and medicine, Asclepius really comes from the Egyptian Imhotep.

Now, Emery knew that people had made pilgrimages to Saqqara. He saw lots of pots on the surface. Pilgrims tend to drop pots and break them along routes. He knew that people came to Saqqara for healing—it was like a lure of the ancient world—and he believed they were making a pilgrimage to the tomb of Imhotep. So Emery started excavating where he thought was a likely site, where he saw these pots, and he dug down, and he hit a tunnel looking very much in size like a subway. That tunnel was filled with mummified birds, ibises more than a million. These were offerings that pilgrims had brought to Imhotep. When Imhotep became a god, the bird that was associated with him was an ibis, so Emery knew he was on the trail of Imhotep's tomb. So he started following these millions of ibises through the tunnels. He had difficulty. Sometimes the roof would cave in and he would have to shore it up.

For years Emery excavated at Saqqara, looking for the tomb of Imhotep. Eventually he even found inscriptions to Imhotep, saying, "Please heal me." You would bring an ibis, give it to a priest and say, "Say a prayer for me. Give it to Imhotep and let my leg be healed." So Emery found this trail and followed it for years, but then he died. He never found the tomb of Imhotep, and it's never been found. No one has picked up the excavation. No one has followed it through, and it could be that he was on the trail, that perhaps the architect of the first pyramid in history is waiting there to be discovered soon, but that's the Step Pyramid of Zoser and his architect, Imhotep.

Now, remember, the kings of the First Dynasty had these dual burials at Abydos and at Saqqara. Zoser had two burials. He had the Step Pyramid, but he had what was also called the southern burial. Just a couple of hundred yards away south of the Step Pyramid is another burial called the southern burial. It's a mastaba-like burial, not a pyramid. It's rather beautiful, by the way—I've been in it. It's a little bit dangerous to go in, it's locked, but it's rather beautiful. It's underground, you go down, and in the burial chamber are beautiful green tiles. It's almost like bathroom tiles. They are lining the wall, and they show Zoser running in the *heb-sed* festival. He is celebrating his jubilee, his thirtieth jubilee, being rejuvenated forever. These tiles are made of faience.

Faience is a kind of ceramic that was an invention in Egypt. It's called "faience," by the way, because of an Italian town, Faenza, that makes similar things nowadays, in modern times. It's ceramic-like. It's a quartzite paste, and when you fire it, when you heat it in a kiln, whatever impurity is inside the paste comes to the surface and glazes it. So, for example, if you put a little malachite in, you can make it green. If you put a little blue turquoise you can make it blue. You can control the color by putting the impurity in the quartzite paste and firing it. So it's a self-glazing ceramic, rather beautiful, and Zoser's southern burial is covered with these tiles, rather elegant, and this is the very first pyramid subsidiary burial. You have a pyramid and a second burial.

Zoser starts the pyramid tradition, and it's continued by his successor, and his successor's pyramid is one of the funniest stories in archaeology. It's called, well, his name is Horus Sekhemkhet. The Pharaoh Horus Sekhemkhet was going to build a step pyramid just like Zoser's, but he died before it was finished. It was only a couple of meters high. The pyramid was discovered as late as 1951. What was great about it was, sure, it was unfinished—it only went a few meters high—but two things were wonderful about it. One is because it was unfinished we could tell something about how pyramids were built. See, always I feel that an unfinished monument is more interesting than a completed one because you can see how they were doing it. You can see where they left off.

And what surprises me is the walls of the pyramid, made out of stone, are still rough. They haven't been finished at the quarry. They were going to be finished inside. You build up the wall, and it's kind of a rough surface, and then a workman would come in and chisel away and make it finished. I would have thought they would finish all the blocks to a uniform standard and then ship them to the site because then you don't have to ship so much stone—what you have is a lighter block. But, no, they shipped rough blocks to the site, put them in place, and then finished them on the site.

But the amazing thing about this pyramid is it was found intact. He died before it was finished, but when the excavators found it the burial chamber was sealed. This was, they hoped, going to be another Tutankhamen's tomb, a pharaoh of the Third Dynasty, his pyramid found unrobbed. So what do you do? Well, they started excavating. They opened a corridor leading down to the burial chamber, and on the floor they found gold bracelets, gold beads, a magical wand, interesting items. Then they came to the burial chamber, which was still sealed, so this was indeed a pyramid that had not been robbed.

Now, I know everybody is wondering, How come I haven't heard about this? How come I haven't heard about this? Well, there is a reason. There is a reason. Because this is after Tutankhamen's tomb, 1950s by the time they are going to open it, everybody was hoping for the greatest treasures ever. So they worked very carefully, and, at the opening of the burial chamber, all the dignitaries in Egypt were called in, all the newsmen were called in, and there was a great opening. They opened the burial chamber, and there in the middle of the burial chamber was a sarcophagus, a stone sarcophagus, still sealed.

Now, let me say something about a sarcophagus, what a sarcophagus is. It's different from a coffin. It's stone. A coffin is usually made out of wood. And the reason sarcophagi are always stone—the word comes from the Greek. When the Greeks first came into Egypt and opened some of these stone sarcophagi, they looked inside, and what they found were badly preserved mummies, basically skeletons. They looked at the skeletons that were inside these stone sarcophagi, and they called them "flesh eaters," sarcophagi, as in "esophagus," sarcophagus. They are flesh eaters. That's what sarcophagi means, "flesh eaters." So they called these stone sarcophagi "flesh eaters."

So when they opened this burial chamber there was a sarcophagus, still sealed, intact. On top of it were some burnt plants, probably a funerary wreath, probably a funerary wreath that had been burned as an offering. Everybody was waiting to see the body of Horus Sekhemkhet. The lid was difficult; it was really a tense situation. The lid was very difficult to lift. It was not a lid that came off the top of the sarcophagus. It was a lid on the side of the sarcophagus that had to be lifted up by police. It was a very difficult operation, but they finally lifted it off—and nobody was home. There was no Horus Sekhemkhet in it. It was empty.

Now, why would a pharaoh build a pyramid, put gold jewelry in the corridor on the floor, have a sarcophagus, place it in a burial chamber, sealed, with even a funerary wreath on it, and not be buried in it? What was going on? Well, there are a couple of theories. One possibility, of course, is that he is following in the footsteps of Zoser and the kings of the First Dynasty and he was going to have two burials and this is the cenotaph, the false burial, but it's pretty elaborate for a false burial. The other theory is that it was intended to throw off tomb robbers, that Horus Sekhemkhet was afraid that robbers would one day see his pyramid and crash in and take whatever he was buried with and his mummy also. So what he did was he created this as a decoy to fool the robbers, to throw them off the track.

But it didn't work, and I'll tell you why it didn't work. Usually the tomb robbers were the men who built the tombs. They knew the ins and outs of tombs, and they would know what was placed inside the tomb. The workers, if they were working on Horus Sekhemkhet's pyramid, would know that, oh, the pharaoh is not in there, we're doing this as a dummy. Whoever seals that knows nothing is in there. They had never seen the pharaoh's body brought in, they knew that it was a dummy, and they left it alone. The interesting thing, though, is we still don't know where Horus Sekhemkhet was buried. He must have another tomb. If this was the decoy, if this is the one to throw off the tomb robbers, there is another burial somewhere, but we haven't found that one yet.

What we've seen in this beginning of what we call the Old Kingdom is Egypt rise to greatness where a pharaoh named Zoser can build the greatest building on the planet, the Step Pyramid of Saqqara, and this is a tradition that will be continued, and we'll talk about that next time.

Lecture Eight
Sneferu, the Pyramid Builder (2613–2589 B.C.)

Scope:

This lecture will present a portrait of the founder of the "Fabulous Fourth" Dynasty, Sneferu. We will see how a pharaoh became king—by marrying the right woman! Sneferu's reign saw three major innovations: (1) by trial and error, true pyramid construction began; (2) Egypt became an international power; and (3) artistic standards were established that would last for thousands of years.

Outline

I. Sneferu (2613–2589 B.C.) built several pyramids, a great architectural achievement. He was the first pharaoh we know of who carved his name in a cartouche.

  A. Meidum is the first attempt at a true pyramid. It looks more like a tower than a pyramid.

    1. A stepped pyramid was first built, the steps later filled in with limestone. But the limestone casing wasn't stable, and the pyramid seems to have been abandoned.

    2. There was a temple next to the pyramid.

    3. The pyramid's burial chamber, which had a vaulted ceiling, was the first to be built above ground.

    4. A corbelled ceiling in the chamber prevented collapse by distributing the weight of the huge stones in the pyramid.

    5. Two uninscribed stelae nearby, however, suggest that the pyramid was never used. Some graffiti for Sneferu can still be seen in the mortuary temple, the only hard evidence we have that it is his pyramid.

  B. The Bent Pyramid of Dahshur was Sneferu's second pyramid.

    1. Why the bend? It starts out like Meidum at 54 degrees. The corners of the pyramid were built on unstable ground, so structural changes were necessary.

    2. The burial chamber was probably the greatest room in the world, with a spectacular vaulted ceiling that was 55 feet high.

3. But there were problems—cracks formed because the pyramid was not stable at the corners. Cedar beams were used to brace the collapsing walls. The pyramid was quickly finished with a "bend" in the angle.
   4. This pyramid, nearly as large as the Great Pyramid at Giza, also had to be abandoned.
   5. A Valley Temple and causeway completed the complex.
   C. The Red Pyramid of Dahshur, a third pyramid, is Sneferu's burial place. Fully complete, it is the first large true pyramid.

II. Sneferu's international policies took him beyond the borders of Egypt.
   A. Cedars of Lebanon, obtained through trade, were needed for ships and temple doors.
      1. Wood was a scarce commodity in Egypt; thus, stone buildings were common.
      2. From river boats to sacred barques, ships were central to Egypt. But Egyptians were not good sailors, spoiled as they were by the prevailing winds when sailing up the Nile or the current when sailing down it. They called the Mediterranean "the great green." A trip to Lebanon for cedars was a big matter.
   B. Sneferu sent expeditions to Sinai to mine turquoise, an exotic commodity for jewelry.
      1. Inscriptions call Sneferu "Smiter of Barbarians" in the foreign territory. He had a large army to get what he wanted in the Sinai.
      2. There were many difficulties in mining: the organization for such a trip was considerable in itself, not to mention the demands made by the terrible summer heat.
      3. The Temple of Serabit el-Khadim was built like a mine on top of a mountain dedicated to Hathor, "Our Lady of Turquoise." Flinders Petrie excavated the temple and found a small sphinx, which he later buried for protection without ever marking where he put it.

III. The art of Sneferu's reign set standards for centuries to come.
   A. His wife had beautiful inlaid turquoise jewelry.
   B. The first great life-size portrait statues were sculpted during his reign.

1. Those of Rahotep (high priest of Memphis) and Nofret are masterpieces.
2. Hemiunu, a pyramid architect and son of Sneferu, is depicted as fat, a sign of prosperity.

IV. Papyrus Westcar, in Berlin, contains the first personal anecdote about a king.
   A. The papyrus shows the first use of exotic fishnet clothing—young ladies in fishnet attire are described rowing Sneferu.
   B. One rowing girl loses her turquoise fish amulet.
   C. Sneferu calls a magician who parts the waters for him—centuries before Moses—and the king retrieves the amulet for the girl.
   D. The story is fictional but an indication nonetheless that he was an approachable pharaoh.

V. Sneferu established a family tradition, perhaps his greatest legacy of all.
   A. He built the largest building in the history of the world to that time, the Bent Pyramid.
   B. But Sneferu wasn't deterred by failure, showing his people by example how to build a true pyramid.
   C. He showed Egypt how to be an international power and established artistic conventions.
   D. Khufu (Cheops), his son, who would build the Great Pyramid of Giza, was perhaps his most important legacy of all.

Essential Reading:
I. E. S. Edwards, *The Pyramids of Egypt*, Chapters 2 and 3.

Questions to Consider:
1. What were the stages in the development of the true pyramid?
2. Other than pyramids, what were Sneferu's achievements?

Lecture Eight—Transcript
Sneferu, The Pyramid Builder (2613–2589 B.C.)

Welcome back. Remember last time how we saw the first pyramid ever built, the Step Pyramid at Saqqara? Well, what I want to do today is I want to take you through to the true pyramid, the great pyramids that we all think about. Now, I'm kind of happy about this lecture, more than any other, because I get to talk about my favorite pharaoh, somebody you probably never heard about: Sneferu. He's the one who taught Egypt how to build the pyramids.

Now, one of the things that people don't quite understand is they didn't just build pyramids. They didn't get it right from the beginning. There were disasters. There are pyramids in the deserts that collapsed while they were being built, and Sneferu is the one who sort of endured the disasters and figured out how to get it right. But he did more than that. He also made Egypt an international power. The third great thing he did was he set artistic standards that were going to last for thousands of years. So, to me, Sneferu is the greatest pharaoh that ever lived.

Let me start with our Step Pyramid and build up. Remember that the Step Pyramid was just kind of architectural progression. First we had burials in the sandpits. Then eventually that didn't work, so people were buried in rock-cut tombs in the ground so the sand wouldn't wash away, wouldn't be blown away. Then somebody got the idea of, okay, bury them in a rock pit but put a benchlike structure called a mastaba, a little chapel, over it, kind of decorative, where people can go and have a meal, pay their respects. Then Imhotep, the architect for the Step Pyramid, got the idea of putting a mastaba on top of a mastaba on top of a mastaba for his Pharaoh Zoser, so you get a wedding cake-type pyramid, the Step Pyramid of Saqqara, the first building in stone in the history of the world.

Now, still it's that same basic burial—the pharaoh is underground in a rock pit—but now we have a fancy mastaba, the Step Pyramid. But it's not yet a true pyramid. We don't yet have those pyramids that we all think of, the ones with the nice smooth sides. It's Sneferu who is going to show you how to do that one. Let me tell you a little bit about him.

First, he's my favorite pharaoh, but the thing that bothers me about him (there is only one thing that bothers me about him) is we have a few portraits of him and he looks a little bit like a nerd. He has this receding chin; he doesn't look like the strong, great pharaoh. There is a wonderful monument of him, not a complete monument—it's a stela—and by now you know that a stela is this round-topped stone carving, and it's right outside in the garden of the Egyptian Museum in Cairo. Most tourists just walk by it. They are eager to get into the museum and see the objects, Tutankhamen's treasures, but it's standing right out there.

If you go look to the left, you'll see Sneferu there carved on a stela with his little receding chin, but you'll see more. Sneferu was also the first pharaoh that we're sure of who carved his name in a cartouche, that oval that represents the king's dominion over the land. In a sense the cartouche, that oval encircling the pharaoh's name, is a magical circle. Encircling was a notion that these Egyptians used quite a bit of magic. It was protective. So we've got the pharaoh's name in a cartouche. Sneferu is an innovator; he's going to do some new things, and it's a wonderful little stela outside the Egyptian Museum. When you go there, look left and you'll see it. He's the pharaoh who attempts the first true pyramid.

Now, the first pyramid that he built, and he built several—he's not just a one-pyramid pharaoh—the first pyramid that he built is called the Meidum Pyramid. It's the town where it is. As soon as you see it you know that there is something wrong. It doesn't look right. It looks more like a tower, a medieval tower. It's certainly not a pyramid shape. It's got a large pile of sand at the base. By large I mean it's like 50, 100 feet high almost. It looks like the thing collapsed. It looks like there is just something wrong. Now, Sneferu intended it as a true pyramid, and let me tell you how he started to build it.

He built a step pyramid just like Zoser, but then he decided to fill in the steps with beautiful white limestone, trying to create a true pyramid, but it didn't work. When excavators looked at this pyramid carefully, there was never any indication that it was ever used. It seems to have been abandoned. Why? One theory is that the limestone casing they used to try to encase the pyramid was slipping. It wasn't stable. It wasn't tied in enough to the body of the pyramid. It was too smooth and started to slip, and the pyramid had to be abandoned. The Meidum Pyramid is the first attempt at a true pyramid, but it's not just a pyramid. There is more than just that. It's a pyramid complex.

He innovates things that are going to be used by the next pharaohs. There is a causeway, a long passageway that leads down to the valley, and in the valley Sneferu had a temple built which we call the valley temple. There are many pyramids that have valley temples. We're not 100 percent sure of the reason for that valley temple, but I think the reason is that's where the pharaoh's body was mummified. So imagine the ceremonies that took place. The pharaoh's body is mummified in a temple in the valley. Then by a sacred ceremony it's brought up the causeway, and the causeway was a narrow passageway maybe seven or eight feet wide, that's all, maybe a little bit more, and it's about seven feet high, with a roof over it. So priests are carrying the body of the pharaoh to the pyramid for burial.

Now, the mortuary temple as we call it, is right next to the pyramid, and it's an interesting monument, a mortuary temple. The mortuary temple was used by the pharaoh so that priests could come and make offerings to his soul forever. It was a place where you could leave food offerings. So he's got a valley temple where his body is mummified, a causeway, right next to the pyramid, and a mortuary temple. It's quite a bit of a complex. It's not just a simple pyramid.

The pyramid itself has innovations that are way ahead of its time. First, this is the first aboveground burial in a pyramid. Remember, Zoser, the builder of the Step Pyramid, is still buried underground. He's just got this Step Pyramid wedding cake above him. Sneferu decides to have his body buried above the ground. So, for the pyramid, you go into the pyramid, and you go down more than 100 feet into the bedrock, and then you climb up a little stairway, and there is a burial chamber. Sneferu intended to be buried in that burial chamber aboveground. It creates an architectural problem that had to be solved.

Think about this. The pharaoh's body is inside the pyramid now but towards the bottom of the pyramid. You've got millions of pounds of stone on the ceiling of the burial chamber. How do you roof over a large area? How do you roof over something, say, the size of a living room with a million pounds of stone above it? You can't put a slab of granite across the ceiling and have that as your ceiling because that will crack. What do you do? Well, he solved it by what we call a corbeled ceiling. What he did in the burial chamber is he took stones and he built up the walls of stones, and each layer of stone moves inward a little bit. It moves inward and inward and inward, creating what we call a corbeled ceiling, until you get to the top. It looks a little bit like an arch made out of steps, stepping in, in, in, until at the top you only have an inch or two for the last block at the very top. So all the weight of the pyramid doesn't come down on one big slab; it's distributed through the pyramid.

A corbeled ceiling is a clever way of doing this. Sneferu solved that problem. It's the first aboveground burial ever for a pharaoh, but as I said, the pyramid wasn't used. He had two stelae erected, those large, stone, round-topped things that were supposed to be inscribed, and they are still there. They are still right there by the mortuary temple, but they are uninscribed. They were never used. That's one way we're pretty sure that this pyramid was never used because he would have had inscriptions with his name all over the place. The casing stones probably started slipping, they realized the pyramid was unstable, and it was abandoned.

Let me tell you a curious thing about this pyramid and other pyramids. It's a tremendous effort to build a pyramid—manpower, social organization—and we'll talk about that later, but how come they are never inscribed? If you go inside the pyramid of Meidum, there are no inscriptions. There is no way in the world that you could tell that this was Sneferu's pyramid. He didn't put his name on it, didn't claim it. Maybe the stela would have done that, but there are no inscriptions. The only reason we know this is Sneferu's pyramid, the only reason, is that there is graffiti on the wall of the mortuary temple, old graffiti, 18th Dynasty graffiti, roughly the time of King Tutankhamen a thousand years later. A priest came to the temple, and he said, "I came to the temple of Sneferu, found the sun shining in it, and it was beautiful." Only because of this inscription are we pretty sure that this was Sneferu's pyramid.

Now what does Sneferu do? He's built a pyramid, and it's unusable. He starts another pyramid. The next pyramid he builds is at a place called Dahshur. Now, Dahshur has the second pyramid that Sneferu built. It's called the Bent Pyramid. It's called the Bent Pyramid because it starts out at a nice angle, and when he gets to the top it bends. It looks like they changed the plan all of a sudden, and it bends at the top. Why does it bend at the top? Well, I'll give you an answer. They had problems with this pyramid, too, major problems.

A pyramid is not built on sand. That's your first rule of pyramid building: Sand shifts; it's unstable. You build it on bedrock. The corners of the Bent Pyramid were built on unstable ground, and what happened was they started shifting and the pyramid starting moving inward.

Now, let me tell you about what's inside this pyramid, this Bent Pyramid. I've been in it; it is very dangerous. It is the most dangerous thing I've ever done, going to the burial chamber of Sneferu. You go down this long, descending passageway, more than 100 feet down, and then to get up to the burial chamber you climb a ladder that is 55 feet high. The burial chambers (there are actually two burial chambers in this pyramid), the burial chamber was probably the greatest room ever built on the planet by the time it was built. It is 55 feet high with a corbeled ceiling going all the way up for 55 feet. It's a huge room, the largest enclosed room probably ever built up until that time. But, as I said, the corners were unstable.

When you look inside that burial chamber, you get a shock. It's filled with cedar beams. There are huge beams going from wall to wall, holding the walls apart. The walls have huge cracks in them. What happened, because the corners were shifting, the weight of the pyramid starting coming inward, imploding on the wall, cracking the wall. The wall started to move inward, and to keep it from totally collapsing inward they brought in cedars of Lebanon to hold the walls apart. Then, what I figure they did was—this pyramid isn't going to work either, his second disaster; it's got to be abandoned; it's not stable—they decided to finish it anyway, but to finish it quickly they put a bend at the top because it requires less stone, they could do it faster, and they simply abandoned it. Sneferu's second pyramid was abandoned.

Now, this is a large pyramid. It's nearly as large as the Great Pyramid at Giza. This is not a small affair. It's a couple hundred feet high. But Sneferu was not going to give up. This pyramid at Dahshur, the Bent Pyramid, also has a valley temple. It has a causeway, it had everything, but it couldn't be used.

What does Sneferu do? He goes a mile away, still at Dahshur, and builds a third pyramid, the Red Pyramid. The Red Pyramid is called the Red Pyramid because when it shines in the sun, when the sun is on it shining, it looks a little bit red. So Sneferu starts a third pyramid, and he completes it, and that's where Sneferu was buried.

This is the first large true pyramid in the history of the world. It's really Sneferu who showed the world how to build pyramids—by trial and error, though. There were disasters, there were problems, but Sneferu just didn't give up. He was an incredible pharaoh.

Pyramid building was only one of the things he did. He made Egypt an international power, and let me tell you about that. First, remember when he had to bring in cedars of Lebanon to keep the walls apart inside that collapsing pyramid. He had to go to Lebanon to get it. Now, remember, Egypt is not a tree-rich country. There are no forests in Egypt, but they needed wood, always, for Nile boats. They needed the wood for boats, so you had to get wood somewhere, and Lebanon was the place to get the cedar. Sneferu organized expeditions, trading expeditions. They didn't pillage and plunder but went on trading expeditions to Lebanon to get cedar for these boats. It wasn't just for boats, though. He needed great cedars of Lebanon for doors to temples. He needed cedars of Lebanon for the flagpoles that were in front of temples. There was plenty of need for cedar, and Sneferu did it via international expeditions. The first one we're really sure that goes into international realms—that was Sneferu.

Let me say a little bit about boats in ancient Egypt. If you wanted to travel any long distance in Egypt and you had a little bit of wealth, you went by boat. It was the only way to do it. We see lots of representations of boats on the walls of Egyptian tombs and temples. But let me say this right out in front, statement of fact, the Egyptians were terrible sailors. They weren't really skilled at sailing because they were spoiled by the Nile. It was a very easy navigation to do. You see, the current always flows from south to north.

The reason a river flows in one direction rather than the other is simply plate tectonics. The plate simply slipped under when the earth was being formed. The plate is under, and water just flows downhill. So the Nile flows always south to north. The prevailing wind is always north to south. So if you're going one way—say you're going up the river—you put up your sails, you've got the wind at your back, you're sailing along. If you're coming home, you can put down your sails, put in your oars for steering, and you're going home. It's easy. As a matter of fact, if you look at tomb paintings, you can tell if a boat is going north or south by whether its sails are up. It's a kind of neat thing.

But this spoiled the Egyptians. They really weren't good sailors. They never liked to go out on the Mediterranean, for example. Never. I mean, they called the Mediterranean, "the *waj-wer*," "the great green." It was like this: "Wu." When they did trading expeditions, that was really a bold thing. So for Sneferu to go to Lebanon to get cedars was a big deal, a really big deal, but he had this kind of international idea. He was not afraid of going beyond the borders of Egypt.

And let me tell you about some other things he did. He sent mining expeditions to the Sinai. Now, the Sinai was foreign land. Why go to the Sinai? They had turquoise. Turquoise was not found in Egypt. No, it's in the Sinai. It was a beautiful blue stone that they liked for jewelry. So it's Sneferu who sends an expedition to the Sinai. This was a major thing to do. First of all, this was barbarian territory, this was foreign territory. You had to have an army, and Sneferu had an army. All along the Sinai he carved inscriptions of himself, and you know what it says? It shows Sneferu in that smiting pose, the same as the Narmer Palette, right hand up with the mace (the rock on a stick) in his hand, ready to smite the enemy. It shows him ready to smite an enemy, and it says, "Sneferu, smiter of barbarians." So he went with an army.

When you went to the Sinai, though, this was a tough, tough expedition. You had to have boats to go across, so you needed boats, you needed organization, and sometimes there were expeditions that went in the summer, which is incredibly hot. There are inscriptions in the Sinai from Sneferu's men. They say, "The mountain branded our skin." It was so hot working in the turquoise mines. Working turquoise is very difficult. You follow a vein through a little tunnel. I mean, you're often on your belly just carving away at little bits of turquoise.

I'll never forget going into the Sinai about, it must be 20 years ago. I wanted to see Sneferu's turquoise mines, just wanted to see them. I went to the Sinai, and I talked to the locals. I asked some Bedouin, "Where are the turquoise mines?" They said, "Oh, come on. We'll go show you." A guy hops in a jeep, goes with me, and it's this little tunnel going into the mountain. I mean, I had to crawl in on my belly. And the Bedouin said to me, "The miner is in there now. His name is Solom." I'll never forget, a little old man. So we go inside, and I yell, "Solom!" and he comes out, a little old man, a tiny man.

We were talking in Arabic, and I said to him, "Do you have any turquoise?" I was with quite a few of my students; we were going on this kind of little expedition. And I said, "Do you have any turquoise?" and he said, "Yes." I said, "Gee, could we buy some?" He said, "Sure." So he takes out of his pocket maybe six or seven little chunks of turquoise—little, little bits. I asked him, "How much are they?" The whole probably came to the equivalent of a dollar, and he gives them to me, and I said to him, "How do you make a living?" He said, "Well, I go in the turquoise mine, and I take out the turquoise, and I put it in a box, and once a month a friend of mine takes a bus, he goes to Cairo, and he sells it in the bazaar in Cairo."

How much could the man make? I have no idea, next to nothing. And I said to him—I was curious—I said, "Solom, why do you do this? You really don't make a lot of money." And his answer just blew me away. He said, it's translated from the Arabic, but basically he said to me, "Who wants a nine-to-five job?" What he meant was, and I asked him, he said, "You know, the people with the goats—they have to get up every morning and bring them to the pastureland. They have to take care of them." He said, "I'm free. If I one day don't want to get out of bed, I don't have to get out of bed." That's a turquoise miner, probably the last turquoise miner in the Sinai.

But the inscriptions are really quite something, and the turquoise mines go up and down a mountain, and sometimes you have to go way up a mountain and then tunnel in. It was a very, very dangerous expedition; many people died. And you know what Sneferu did, which was really kind of neat? On top of the mountain there is a temple for the miners to worship at, and it's dedicated to Hathor, the goddess Hathor who is sometimes shown as a cow-headed goddess. Her name was "Our Lady of Turquoise" there. She was the patron saint of the turquoise miners. So Sneferu really was not afraid of sending expeditions out into the foreign lands.

This site, this temple on top of a mountain, has a name. I don't know what it means. It's Arabic, Serabit el-Khadim. That's what the Arabs call it; the locals call it that. It was excavated by Flinders Petrie, our man Petrie. Petrie found, when he was excavating, a sphinx, a small sphinx maybe five feet long at the most. But he couldn't get it down from the mountain, and he didn't want to leave it there because he was afraid it would be broken. So he buried it up on top of the mountain, but he never put the "X" on the map that marks where this sphinx is. So some day some excavator is going to find a sphinx from the top of Serabit el-Khadim in the Sinai.

Sneferu did great things, really wonderful things. Let me tell you about some other things. He also set the standards for art. During Sneferu's reign he created jewelry that nobody else had ever seen. His wife had beautiful turquoise jewelry, inlays like in the shape of butterflies, from the turquoise mines. This was the most fashionable thing you could see. But he also had statues of his children made, life-size statues out of stone that are spectacular. They are the masterpieces of Egyptian art, and they come at the beginning of the history of art. These were things that artists would shoot for for the next centuries after. There is a wonderful one in the Egyptian Museum of Rahotep, who was a priest of Memphis, his son, and his wife Nofret.

Now what's really wonderful is they are realistic. They are life-size; they are full size, beautifully painted; and they have rock crystal eyes, so the eyes actually look real; and the details are just perfect. If you look at the hair of Nofret you will see that she's wearing a wig. Wealthy Egyptian women often wore wigs made of human hair, fairly large, like big hair, and they would put it over their natural hair. If you look at Nofret you can see she's wearing a wig, and what they've shown is, on her forehead is her natural hair peaking out. Lovely little details.

Some of his Sneferu's were represented in these full life-size statues, and what's neat about the sons is that they are all shown as fat. For example, take Hemiunu, who was an architect and a vizier. (See, Sneferu knew what to do. He was putting all the power, keeping it in his family. His viziers, the prime ministers of Egypt, and the architects who built the other pyramids—they were all his sons.) If you look at Hemiunu, he's got rolls of fat, and that wasn't a bad thing. That was a sign of prosperity. That showed you could afford to eat well. In others, Ankh-haf is also shown. He's bald and fat, really paunchy—this is success. But these are beautiful, realistic statues, and Sneferu is the one who showed Egypt how to do the statues, too, how to set standards for sculptures that would last for thousands of years.

But that's not all. Sneferu is the pharaoh about whom we have the first personal anecdote. We know a little bit about his personality even. I mean, he comes alive for me. I really feel I know who the guy was. There is a papyrus in Berlin called Papyrus Westcar. It's just a story, but I think it tells something about Sneferu. It's a magical papyrus—it has magical stories—and it tells the story of Sneferu being bored one day. His prime minister says to him, "You know, why don't you go rowing? Have the ladies of the court take you rowing, and to cheer you up let's just give them fishnet dresses." This is the first use of exotic fishnet dresses. So he was going to have these handmaidens rowing him on the Nile in his boat to kind of cheer him up—he was bored—and they did it.

The young ladies are in their fishnet dresses, they are rowing Sneferu, and one of the young women is wearing a pendant around her neck, and it's a turquoise fish amulet. Turquoise? She's à la mode—it's the newest thing, a real treasure right from the mines. She leans over the ship just to kind of look down, and it falls off her neck. She starts crying, she's lost her amulet, and Sneferu, he's the king of Egypt, a god on earth, he stops, he says, "What's the matter?" She explains, "I've lost my amulet, my turquoise amulet," and Sneferu says, "Don't worry. I'll get you another amulet." She says, "No, I want my turquoise amulet."

Now, think of that. This young woman is saying to the pharaoh, "No, I want my turquoise amulet." There is a sense that this pharaoh was approachable, he was a good guy. He wasn't sort of this domineering pharaoh. So what does Sneferu do? He calls a magician who comes and parts the waters. (Now, this is like Exodus but a thousand years before Exodus.) We have a story of the waters being parted. There on a rock is the turquoise fish amulet. The magician fetches it and gives it back to the girl. She stops crying, continues rowing, and life goes on.

It's a fiction, of course. It didn't really happen, but I think from this you get a little bit of a sense that Sneferu was an approachable pharaoh. He was somebody that you could talk to. I just like the guy. When I think about his personality, I think about the idea that he just didn't quit. Think about that. He built one pyramid, Meidum. It's abandoned—the casing stones perhaps aren't tied in well enough. Then he goes on to build the largest building in the history of the world at that time, the Bent Pyramid, and it starts imploding. It won't work. Now, at this point he's running out of time. He's probably fairly elderly, and he knows that he's got to get it right or he's not going to have a burial place. He doesn't give up. He doesn't go for some small tomb. He builds a third pyramid. This is a sense of a man that is fearless. That's why he's my favorite pharaoh.

Now, think about what Sneferu has done. He has shown Egypt how to build the pyramids, the first one to get it right for a true pyramid, the first true pyramid. He's built actually three pyramids: three, twice the volume of the Great Pyramid. He's then taken Egypt and made it an international power. He has gone to Lebanon for cedar. He goes into the Sinai for turquoise. Then he establishes artistic conventions and standards that are going to be—I mean, many people feel they were never met again. Many people feel that the art of Sneferu's era is the best art that Egypt ever produced. It's an incredible legacy for one man.

But he's got still one more legacy. What may be Sneferu's greatest legacy is his son, Khufu, who builds the Great Pyramid at Giza, and that's what we'll talk about next time.

Lecture Nine
The Great Pyramid of Giza

Scope:

Here we will learn the "nuts and bolts" of pyramid building. Step by step we will see how a pyramid was built, from leveling the foundation to laying the capstone. Higher mathematics was not needed to build a pyramid, only great care, an endless supply of stone, lots of cheap labor, and a remarkable social organization. We will also discuss the significance of the "Boat Beneath the Pyramid"—the 144-foot boat discovered in 1954 in a pit near the Great Pyramid.

Outline

I. Khufu (2589–2566 B.C.), or Cheops, as the Greeks called him, the son of Sneferu, built the Great Pyramid.

    A. The Great Pyramid is 480 feet high, the highest building in the world until the Eiffel Tower was built. The base covers 13 1/2 acres and is built of 2 1/2 million blocks, averaging 2.5 tons each. It required masses of labor and advanced social organization to build—but not higher mathematics.

    B. The building of the pyramid is burdened with myth and legend.

        1. People talk about the magical power of the pyramidal shape. But its shape was more the result of evolving accidents than a sudden discovery. The pyramid was a tomb for the pharaoh; it wasn't a form that even the ancient Egyptians considered magical.

        2. Napoleon was said to have gone into the burial chamber alone and come out again ashen-faced, refusing to describe what he saw. Was he genuinely disturbed by the experience—or was he just creating the legend of Napoleonic greatness?

        3. Herodotus says 90,000 men at a time built the Great Pyramid in three-month stints, probably in the season when their fields were under water. When he says they used "machines" to build it, however, he's probably referring to levers.

        4. Contrary to popular belief, slaves didn't build the pyramid—the Exodus of the Israelites was much later.

There were never large numbers of slaves doing public works in Egypt.

II. No architectural papyri exist explaining how to build temples or pyramids; it was apparently a trade secret. So how was the pyramid built?

A. Workers cleared the sand down to bedrock. They probably built channels in the earth at the base and filled them with water until they had a level surface, much like the principle of a carpenter's level.

B. The rock quarries were next to the pyramid, so moving stone over long distances was unnecessary.

C. The pyramid has two entrances; visitors today enter by the one that robbers created.

D. The pyramid's original plan changed from a below-ground burial to a higher chamber.

E. The Grand Gallery, a passageway to the burial chamber, is an engineering marvel: a 28-foot high, corbeled ceiling that goes all the way up the pyramid. Its function is unknown.

F. The sarcophagus of Khufu is the only thing in the burial chamber. But it happens to be two inches wider than the doorway! It must have been placed there before the pyramid was finished, and the chamber was built around it.

G. Relieving chambers were used instead of corbeling to remove the weight from the burial chamber ceiling.

H. How were the stones positioned at the top of the pyramid, by ramp or winding road?

1. We know they used ramps elsewhere. Or they may have had the equivalent of a switchback.

2. In the end, careful measurement, not higher mathematics, was "all" that was required for construction. Construction was completed within the 22 years of Khufu's reign.

III. Overall, highly sophisticated social organization was needed for quarrying the stone, transporting the blocks, and feeding the workers.

IV. Khufu buried a boat ("the Cheops boat") next to his pyramid.

    A. In 1954 a boat pit was discovered carved in the bedrock and covered with blocks.

    B. The boat, made of cedars of Lebanon, was broken down into pieces. It was later reconstructed and found to be 150 feet long.

    C. Given that it had no mast fitting, it wasn't intended to sail.

    D. The oars were too small—model tests reveal that it wasn't rowed.

    E. It may have been a ritual boat to take the pharaoh to the next world. Or, it may have been used—only once—to convey the body of Cheops from the east to the west bank of the Nile.

    F. I'm attempting to build a full-scale replica of the boat and put it on the Nile.

Essential Reading:

I. E. S. Edwards, *The Pyramids of Egypt*, Chapter 3.

Questions to Consider:

1. What was the interior of the Great Pyramid like?

2. Which was more essential in building the Great Pyramid, technology or organizational skills?

Lecture Nine—Transcript
The Great Pyramid of Giza

Welcome back. Remember last time I got a chance to talk about my favorite pharaoh, Sneferu? Well, there were three things I wanted to stress about him. If you remember, one was that he established artistic conventions that would last for a thousand years. The other one was he made Egypt an international power by going off to the Sinai for turquoise, to Lebanon for cedar. But the most important was probably that he showed Egypt how to build the pyramids. He's the one who figured out how to build the first true pyramid.

Today I want to talk about his kid, his son, Khufu, who built the Great Pyramid at Giza. Let me say something about Khufu's name, first of all. He's also called Cheops. So when you hear about the Great Pyramid of Cheops it's the same guy. His mama called him Khufu—that was his Egyptian name—but the Greeks called him Cheops. They corrupted his name. So Cheops and Khufu—it's the same pharaoh.

Let me start by saying that he didn't just build the pyramid. He did other things, too. He also built a huge boat next to his pyramid, and I want to talk about that also. But let's start with the pyramid. Now, let me start by acting like a tour guide. Let me give you some statistics about the Great Pyramid of Giza. Giza, of course, is a suburb of Cairo today. It's a plateau, and on it Khufu/Cheops decided to build his pyramid. It's the largest pyramid ever built. It's 480 feet high. Until the Eiffel Tower was built, it was the largest building on earth. Its base is so large that it covers 13.5 acres. It's made of 2.5 million blocks of stone, and they average about 2.5 tons each. It's an incredible, incredible monument.

But let me emphasize something right from the beginning. It's not the kind of monument that required higher mathematics. It's not a high-tech monument. It required masses of labor and skills of social organization—getting people together to build it—but it didn't require higher mathematics. Now, there are an awful lot of myths about the pyramid, the Great Pyramid: its magical properties, people who have had strange experiences inside it. Let me say a few words about that right from the beginning. First, we know the purpose of the Great Pyramid of Giza. It was a tomb for the burial of a pharaoh, no question about it. The difference, remember, between a tomb and a temple is that a tomb is a place of burial and a temple is a place of worship. This was a tomb.

Now, you hear many stories about the magical properties of a pyramid. For example, I'm sure you've heard that you can put a razor blade inside a pyramid shape and if it's dull it will become sharpened. Or that if you put food inside a small pyramid shape that the food won't decay as quickly as if it were outside. All of these stories about the magical properties of the pyramid are silly. Think about what we've learned in the last two lectures about how a pyramid developed. The Egyptians would have thought it was silly. There was no magical significance to the pyramid shape for the ancient Egyptians.

Let's think about how it developed. Remember, in prehistoric times we had our sandpit burials. They eventually developed into rock-cut burials—you go into the bedrock so the sand won't blow away and reveal the body. Then at some point somebody had the idea of building a little structure on top of that, a mastaba, a benchlike structure. And then, when we get to the Third Dynasty, Imhotep, the architect of Zoser, had the idea of putting a mastaba on top of a mastaba, and then he enlarged it and put a few more mastabas, giving you this wedding cake effect of the Step Pyramid at Saqqara. Then comes Sneferu, my man, and he had the idea of filling in the steps and getting the first true pyramid.

The point I want to make is, the pyramid shape was an architectural development, almost an afterthought, almost an accident of the way tomb building was going. No one sat down and said, "Ooh, this has a magical shape—let's build a pyramid." It developed. It evolved. So this razor sharpening, you know, the magical properties of the pyramid, people sleeping under pyramids—it would have even been silly to the ancient Egyptians.

Now, with that said, let me go on to some other stories about the pyramid, and then I'm going to show you how it was built. I want to go in detail and give you a step-by-step description of how the Great Pyramid was built. But let me just say one thing about Napoleon inside the Great Pyramid first. You'll remember from a much earlier lecture, when I talked about the origins of Egyptology, that Napoleon's expedition to Egypt in 1798 was the beginning of Egyptology.

If you'll remember, Bonaparte was a bit of a scholar, a mathematician of sorts, a member of the French Institute in the Division of Mathematics, and he did indeed visit the Great Pyramid when he was in Egypt. He visited it with some of his men. He did not climb to the top of the Great Pyramid. It's possible to do that. It's now illegal—you need special permission—but it's possible. It's like going up a giant staircase. While his men were climbing to the top, Napoleon walked around it. He made a mental calculation (and he was good at math—there is no doubt about it), and the calculation that he did was, given all the stones, he came to the conclusion you could build a wall around the world. You know, that kind of calculation. He loved to do that.

But the interesting story is he went inside the Great Pyramid. He went inside. He went in with an entourage, several people, and went to the burial chamber, and I'll be talking about the burial chamber later. Eventually he asked if he could be left alone inside the burial chamber. They left him alone. Then he came out, and he looked kind of white when he came out, ashen, and one of his officers said, "Are you okay? What happened?" And Bonaparte said—and this is the story that's been repeated down the ages—he said, "Never mind. You wouldn't believe me," and left. And he never spoke about it.

When he was on St. Helena (you know, he was exiled to St. Helena), he was talking to one of his men, and the man said, "He was about to tell me about it, but he said, 'no,' and never did it." So we really don't know what happened with Napoleon inside the Great Pyramid. Maybe he had some mystical vision. And maybe nothing happened, and he just wanted to kind of create part of his legend. But there are plenty of legends associated with the Great Pyramid that just aren't true.

Let me start with what Herodotus tells about it, our Greek tourist who went to Egypt around 450 B.C. and saw everything and wrote down everything. Now, if you remember, one thing he said about the Great Pyramid which we're certain wasn't true, was that inscribed on the outside of the Great Pyramid were the onions and bread, the amount of food that was needed to feed the workmen. That's certainly not true. Nobody is going to put that on a pyramid. But what Herodotus does tell us about the building of the pyramid—and this is interesting—he says (now, he was told this, of course, and remember he's there in 450 B.C.; the pyramids are almost 2,000 years old), he says he was told that it took 90,000 men working on the pyramid at the same time to build it. It's 90,000 men working, and they worked three months at a time, it seems.

Now, what I think is this. Did they work in shifts, you know, a few months at a time? What happened? Well, the 90,000 men is an interesting figure, and the three months at a time I think is interesting. What probably happened is a theory that I think is maybe the good theory: The pyramids, of course, were built with free labor, no slaves. The Exodus, when we have all the Israelites in Egypt, is much later. There were never a large number of slaves in Egypt that were used for work projects—never. Do you ever watch those movies where you see the pyramids being built, and you've got the slaves hauling on the blocks, and you've got one guy with a whip, whipping the slaves pulling the block? Didn't you ever wonder why the slaves don't just grab this guy and beat him up? There was no weapon in ancient Egypt that gave anybody a great advantage over a large of number of people. It would be very difficult to control thousands of slaves.

We know for a fact that the Great Pyramid of Egypt was built by free labor. We have inscriptions by the work gangs that worked on the pyramid that say, "Khufu's gang did great work" and things like that. So it was built by free labor, and Herodotus says 90,000 men worked on it a few months at a time. Now, what I think he means is this. Egypt was mainly agrarian. Practically everybody was a farmer. And remember that the Nile overflowed its banks each year. One of the seasons in Egypt was called inundation, when the land was inundated with the water. What that meant was there was time when the fields were under water—you couldn't do anything. Then you had a large workforce that you could marshal to work on the pyramid. So I think during inundation you had maybe 90,000 men working on it at one time. You've got the farmers, unskilled labor, everybody pulling together to build this pyramid. That's probably what Herodotus means.

He says something also that's very interesting about the pyramid. He says it was built with machines. Now, of course, this is 450 B.C. What does he mean by a machine? One possibility is levers. The Egyptians to this day have a device called a shaduf. They use a shaduf for raising water from the Nile to the fields. It's a long pole, and at one end it's got a weight. At the other end is the bucket. So the bucket goes down, and then the weight pulls the bucket up with the water in it, and you dump it into the field. You can lift things rather easily. It's a kind of lever and fulcrum system. That's what the Egyptians may have had. What some people have suggested is that they had these levers, these shadufs, so to speak, on each level of the pyramid as they were lifting blocks up, up, and up, and that's what Herodotus may have meant when he said they had machines. But he gives us one of the very few ancient accounts of building anything.

For some reason the ancient Egyptians never wrote down how they built the pyramid. We have no papyrus at all that gives us a clue to how they built the pyramid. Now, I don't mean it's only pyramids that they didn't write down. We have no architectural papyri at all. Think about all the buildings that the Egyptians did. They never wrote down how to build a temple or how to build a pyramid. Never. It may have been a kind of secret among the architects, that they didn't want trade secrets to go out. There were other things they didn't write down. For example, they mummified people for thousands of years, but there was no papyrus that tells us how to mummify a person. These are trade secrets. So if we're going to figure out how the pyramid was built, we have to sort of just look at it and think, and that's what we'll do.

Now, first, when you go on the Giza Plateau there are two pyramids that actually look very similar. It's hard to tell which is the Great Pyramid. One was built by Khufu. That's the one we call the Great Pyramid. That's the tallest one. But there is another pyramid that's only 20 feet shorter built by a successor, Chephren, as he's called by the Greeks. The way you can tell them apart is the one that is not the Great Pyramid still has some of its white limestone casing at the very top. At the very top it's got a little bit of frosting—at the top of the peak. That's how you can tell that that's not the Great Pyramid. Most of that fine white limestone casing was pulled down in the Middle Ages to build the mosques of Cairo. So, if you want to see the really fine white limestone casing of the Great Pyramid, go to the mosques of Cairo. It's called Tura limestone. It came from the Tura quarries.

Now, how do you build a pyramid? First, as you know from the last lecture, you don't build a pyramid on sand. Sand is unstable. It shifts; it moves. You clear down to bedrock, and then what you have to do is level the bedrock. You want it perfectly level. Now, how do you level an area 13.5 acres? The base is 13.5 acres. The prevailing theory is that you use basically something like a carpenter's bubble that you put on top of a bookshelf and you can see if it's level when the bubble is showing. What they probably did is, within those 13 acres, the base, that square base, 13.5 acres, they dug channels, and they filled them with water. Wherever the water would run out you know that that's lower than the rest of the base. So you keep leveling, digging channels, and leveling until the water pretty much stays in. Then you know you've got a level base, like a carpenter.

And it's very level, by the way. There have been very careful surveys done recently of the Great Pyramid's base, and you want to know how level it is? Now, being 13.5 acres from one corner to the other, it never varies by more than two inches over 13.5 acres. That's precision. But let me emphasize: It's precision. It's great workmanship. It's not high tech. You don't need higher mathematics to build a pyramid.

Well, we've got the foundation leveled. What can we say about the inside of the pyramid? How do you bring all these blocks to the site? First of all, you don't have to bring a lot of them to the site. The quarries were right around the pyramid. You can to this day walk around the pyramid and see the quarries. You can see places where stones were pulled out. So a lot of the stonework in the pyramid comes from right around it. That saves transportation costs—you don't have to transport so many blocks. The very finest limestone for the casing, for that smooth outer surface, that came from a little bit of a ways. It was floated across the Nile and then hauled into place.

The inside of the Great Pyramid is a marvel. It really is. By the way, there are two entrances. If you go to the Great Pyramid you will see that there are really two entrances. One entrance is a thieves' entrance. The pyramid's entrance was covered over with the white limestone. Nobody knew where the entrance was, even in ancient times. In the ninth century, the Caliph el-Mamoun—and we hear about him in *The Thousand and One Nights*, the Arabian tales—we hear about him, and it says that he wanted to rob the Great Pyramid but didn't know where the entrance was. So he put workmen chiseling away at the outside of the pyramid, and they kept chiseling and chiseling, and nothing happened. Eventually they tried to do it faster, and what they did was they built fires on the pyramid and doused it with cold water, cracking the stones.

They kept removing stones, removing more stones. They were about to give up when one of the workmen heard a sound inside of a stone falling, so they knew they had hit a hollow chamber. And, according to *The Thousand and One Nights*, they went in and they found not much treasure, just enough treasure to pay the workmen. It's, of course, a story, but probably it is true that in the ninth century or around there they did indeed enter the Great Pyramid. That is the entrance, by the way—the ninth-century robbers' entrance—that tourists go into today. You don't go into the original entrance. That's higher up. That's sealed off. But that's the way that tourists now go in—through where the robbers went in.

Now, what's it like inside the pyramid? Well, the pyramid underwent changes as it was being built. There were changes in the plan. Originally there was going to be a below ground burial. There is an unfinished pit. It goes down. There is a big chamber beneath the ground, unfinished. You can still see the rock, the bedrock, the crude bedrock, unfinished. Khufu's burial was above ground, way up in the pyramid, way up.

Now, how do you get that high up? Well, there is a remarkable, remarkable passageway to get to the burial chamber. It's called the Grand Gallery. It's a room that is still being debated as to what was it used for. It's 28 feet high. It's narrow. It has corbeled roofs again. Remember, Sneferu is the one who figures out to use a corbeled roof. It's 28 feet high and maybe 10 feet wide perhaps, and it goes all the way up the pyramid inside. Nobody knows exactly why it was built. Some people think that they stored blocks in that Grand Gallery that were going to be slid down to seal the entranceway because there are large granite blocks that were slid down and plugged the entranceway.

You go up this Grand Gallery, and then you come to the burial chamber. Now, there are a couple of puzzles about the burial chamber. One, inside the burial chamber is the sarcophagus, the stone sarcophagus of Khufu, the only thing ever found inside the burial chamber. It once had a lid that slid. We can tell that from the sarcophagus, but that's all that's there. No body was found, no inscription in the burial chamber. But that sarcophagus is about two inches wider than the doorway that leads to the burial chamber. It's one piece of stone, the sarcophagus, but it's two inches wider than the doorway. Now, what that means is they put the sarcophagus in the burial chamber before the pyramid was complete. It was probably an attempt to avoid tomb robbing—the robbers couldn't drag the sarcophagus out. So they put it in, and then they built the chamber around it.

The other interesting thing about the burial chamber is the ceiling. You remember that Sneferu, Khufu's father, solved the problem of the roof. How do you build a roof that doesn't crack with the weight of the pyramid above it? By corbeling—steps going inward, inward, inward, all the way to the top of the ceiling. When you go into this burial chamber there is no corbeling. It's big slabs of granite going across the top. How come they don't crack? It's got the weight of the pyramid above it. Well, Khufu took it one further. He had an interesting solution to the problem. It's relieving chambers.

If you could get in, and I've done it (it's not easy—you have to crawl in through a hole outside), if you can get above the burial chamber there is a tiny chamber called a relieving chamber. It's really small. I had to crouch. You can't stand up. You can't even bend over. You really have to kind of crawl in and crouch. It's a chamber that's only about, maybe, four feet high, and that takes some of the pressure off the ceiling. Above that is another relieving chamber, and above that's another relieving chamber. And all the way to the top of that, above the relieving chambers, are two huge blocks of stone forming a triangle, an inverted triangle, like a pyramid sort of. That takes the pressure off the relieving chambers. So all the force of the weight above the pyramid is distributed through the pyramid away from the ceiling. It's a little bit like a corbeled step ceiling, only smoothed out into the form of this inverted "V," a triangle. So the relieving chamber solves the problem of the weight weighing down on the ceiling of the burial chamber so it doesn't collapse.

There are some very interesting questions about the Great Pyramid. How do you get the stones all the way up to the top? It's too steep to pull up a pyramid—how do you do that, a stone weighing maybe three tons? There are two theories. One theory is the ramp theory: that you build a long ramp and the stones are hauled up the ramp, and once you finish the pyramid you remove the ramp. Now, for something the size of the Great Pyramid, going 480 feet up in the air, the ramp would have to be more than a quarter of a mile long. The ramp would be a major engineering project. But we do know they used ramps because, at Karnak Temple, against one of the walls is a mud brick ramp that they used to get blocks up. So maybe they used that technique.

The other possibility is what we call a switchback. It's how, when you go up a mountain road, your car is corkscrewing up the road. It doesn't go straight up the mountain. It goes around and around and around. That's the technique they may have used for getting the blocks up to the top. They may have had the equivalent of a switchback road corkscrewing up around the pyramid until you get the blocks up and then you start filling in. There are two theories. We don't know really which one for sure.

But the point I want to make is it didn't take higher mathematics to do this. It takes careful measurement. For example, another careful measurement: The sides of the Great Pyramid are perfectly aligned on the four compass points: north, south, east, west. Egyptians knew how to do that, by careful observation of the stars. They could do that with the North Star, so you could do that. All of this required great workmanship but not high-tech stuff. For example, some of the limestone casing blocks are still in place. You cannot fit a piece of paper between them, they are so perfectly fitted. That's remarkable. It's wonderful craftsmanship, especially on something that large. And think about it, all of it was done within 22 years, the reign of Khufu—a remarkable achievement.

But I think the amazing achievement is the social organization. You had to have men at the quarries quarrying. You had to have shipping guys. You had to have the guys polishing stones. All of that—coordinating everybody to work on it—that's amazing, especially if you compare it with our society. How often do we undertake a project that we say, "Well, it will take 20 years, but let's see how it goes"? Not very often. That's why you can do great things if you have a pharaoh, a god on earth with absolute power. That's the Great Pyramid of Giza.

Now let me say something about the second thing that I said that Khufu/Cheops achieved: the boat. In 1955, I think it was, '54, probably '54, December '54, a boat was found buried near the Great Pyramid. It was buried in a pit dug into the bedrock, a big pit, a 170-foot pit. It was buried into the bedrock and covered over with limestone blocks, so it was hidden, and it was discovered in 1954. The boat was dismantled. It was like a kit. It wasn't complete, but it was virtually complete in all its pieces—1,500 pieces. It took more than a decade to reassemble the boat. The wood was still in good enough condition, containing enough moisture—the pit had been virtually airtight—that the wood was not brittle, and the entire boat could be reconstructed. It took more than a decade. You can see it today. It's in the boat museum right next to the Great Pyramid. It's in a glass museum.

There are some questions about this boat. It's a beautiful thing. It's absolutely spectacular. It has huge oars and beautiful, graceful lines. It was 150 feet long. It's a big boat and made of cedars of Lebanon, the cedars that Sneferu brought back from his trading expeditions. But there are a couple of questions about this boat. What was it used for? For example, it has no mast. There is no place for a mast for a sail. So it wasn't really a sailing vessel. The oars don't look like they could really function properly. I was wondering about the boat. I was really curious about this boat. I wanted to know, What was it used for?

And one of my students, who is a wonderful model carver, one of the best model carvers probably in the world, worked on this with his father. He carved a test model of this boat. Now, remember, Khufu was also called Cheops. Usually when the boat is referred to it's called the Cheops boat, but don't get confused. It's the same Pharaoh. He carved the model of the Cheops boat, seven feet. It's a pretty big model but to the exact lines. We tested this boat at the Webb Institute for Naval Architecture. They have a large test tank. Before you build the big ship you do a test tank, you know, test it in a tank. We built this little model, seven feet, and put it in the water. Hooked up to the boat are various electrodes, feeding data back to the computers, and we simulated all kinds of conditions: Nile conditions, Mediterranean conditions. We could do it with waves; we could do it with pitch. We could see what it would do. We wanted to see, what was this boat used for? What were its properties?

First, we know it didn't sail because there was no place for a mast. That we know. But what we found out was it had wonderful river properties. It glides through the water beautifully. All the naval architects at the Institute said, "It's beautiful. It's elegant." They were really impressed. But one of the analyses showed that the oars could not possibly propel a boat that size. It didn't have a mast, so the wind didn't propel it. The oars couldn't propel a boat that big.

What was it used for? There are two possibilities. One is that it's a symbolic boat, it's a ritual boat that was supposed to take the pharaoh to the next world. Now, remember, for the long haul you went by boat anytime you went a great distance. The pharaoh was going to go to the next world, which was in the west, across the sky, and this could have been the boat that was going to take Sneferu's son, Khufu, to the next world. The other possibility, and it's the one that I tend to favor, is that the boat was used but only once. It was the boat that, on his last journey, took Khufu from the east bank of the Nile, which is where the living stayed, to the west bank, which is where the pyramids were and the dead were buried. This may have been a boat that was a barge that was towed across the Nile with Khufu's body on it, with Cheops's mummy. Once on the other side of the Nile, the mummy was placed inside the Great Pyramid, and the boat was disassembled and placed in the pit, where it remained for nearly 5,000 years.

There is an interesting construction technique about this boat. It's not nailed together. The Egyptians didn't have nails. When they had to do something with wood they pegged it, but this boat isn't pegged, either. It's what we call a sewn boat. The planks in the boat, and some are 70 feet long, are tied together, but it's still river worthy. What would happen is that the wood would swell and the ropes would shrink, making it watertight. My project that I'm working on right now is to construct a full-scale replica of the boat, a 154-foot boat made in the exact Egyptian way, and put it on the Nile to see just what it could do. The problem right now is to find cedars of Lebanon large enough to get the timber, but we hope to learn a lot.

Lecture Ten
The End of the Old Kingdom

Scope:

This is a period of change and eventual decline. After the fantastic achievements of Dynasty IV, something changed, and Egyptologists are not sure what it was. In addition to building pyramids, pharaohs of Dynasty V seem to have shifted their religious focus to sun worship. And we will see a new architectural development—the sun temples of Abu Gurob. The kings of the next dynasty (Dynasty VI) continue to build pyramids, but these will be small affairs, nothing like the great ones of Sneferu, Khufu, and Chephren. The last king of the dynasty, Pepi II, may have lived too long, been feeble at the end of his reign, and so plunged Egypt into chaos.

Outline

I. There are many curiosities and misconceptions concerning the famous Sphinx, only 20 feet smaller than the Great Pyramid, built in Dynasty IV.

   A. Chephren (2558–2532), or Khafre, carved the Sphinx from a huge rock encountered while building a causeway. It is part *man* in shape (probably Chephren himself), and part lion.

   B. It was built about 4,500 years ago—not in 10,000 B.C., as some geologists have argued.

   C. Napoleon's soldiers didn't shoot away the nose of the Sphinx. We have pre-Napoleonic drawings that show the nose was already missing.

   D. Freudian psychology discusses the Sphinx as a woman—but it's a man wearing a headdress reserved only for royalty. The false beard is missing, parts of which ended up in the British and Egyptian museums. The British Museum, which doesn't display its fragment, probably doesn't want to return it to Egypt for fear of creating a precedent.

   E. Chephren's Valley temple is the only large one from the period. It is paved with alabaster. But after Chephren, things would change.

   F. His successor, Menkaure (Mycerinus), also built on the Giza Plateau, although his pyramid was smaller.

G. The last pharaoh of Dynasty IV, Shepseskaf, moved away from Giza. He returned to Saqqara and built a mastaba. The great pyramid-building era was over.

II. Dynasty V (2498–2345 B.C.) was the time of the solar kings.

    A. Rejecting tradition, the pharaohs built sun temples at Abu Gurob, south of Saqqara, in addition to their pyramids at nearby Abu Sir. The ben-ben stone, atop a squat obelisk, is central at the temples with an altar in front.

    B. The kings changed their names. After Userkaf the pharaohs take *Re* names: Sahure, Neferirkare, Shepseskare, and so on. It may be that the priests are exerting a stronger influence.

    C. Pyramid texts were begun under Unas (2375–2345 B.C.), the last king of Dynasty V. He returned to Saqqara and built a small pyramid inscribed with magical spells. The pyramid texts on the interior walls are intended to ensure that the pharaoh will get to the next world. The inscriptions are in columns—individually done, not stenciled.

        1. The spells, in three stages, were, first of all, supposed to keep the body undisturbed before "going west."

        2. The second stage was to make sure the voyage to the west was finished safely. Associated with the setting sun, the west was a symbol of death in Egyptian thinking.

        3. The third and last stage was to ensure that the pharaoh was accepted into the next world. The spells operated on a magical principle: 'The word is the deed.'

        4. One text, the "cannibal hymn," describes Unas eating the entrails of his enemy. But the meaning may not be literal. E. A. Wallace Budge, curator of the Egyptian collection at the British Museum in the early part of the twentieth century, argued that the story of Osiris was originally offered as a cautionary tale against cannibalism.

III. Dynasty VI (2345–2181 B.C.) was the last Old Kingdom dynasty.

    A. The kings continued to build small pyramids, like hills, inscribed with texts.

B. Mastabas of the nobility rivaled pharaohs' pyramids. Apparently, the nobles' power was increasing at the pharaoh's expense.

C. There was a total collapse at the end of the Old Kingdom, then a recovery leading to the Middle Kingdom, and another collapse before the New Kingdom. As far as I know, Egypt is the only great civilization to endure *two* major collapses.

    1. Pepi II (2278–2184 B.C.) was the last pharaoh of the Old Kingdom.

    2. He ruled for 94 years, the longest reign in the history of the world.

    3. Perhaps he ruled *too* long and became feeble. This is the inherent danger of a pharaoh-centric government. His gradual descent may have led to the collapse of Egyptian civilization.

Essential Reading:

Aidan Dodson, *Monarchs of the Nile*, Chapter V.

Supplementary Reading:

Peter Clayton, *Chronicle of the Pharaohs*, pp. 60–68.

Questions to Consider:

1. What changes do we see in religious buildings during this period?

2. What are the possible causes of the decline of the Old Kingdom?

Lecture Ten—Transcript
The End of the Old Kingdom

Hi. Welcome back. Let me recap a little bit where we left off last time. You remember in the Third Dynasty we saw the first pyramid ever being built, the Step Pyramid of Zoser. Then in the Fourth Dynasty we start to get the true pyramids. We get my man Sneferu building three pyramids, including the first true pyramid ever. Then we ended with Khufu or Cheops, either way, same guy, building the Great Pyramid of Giza. Well, in this lecture I'm going to try to show you where it all goes, and it's mostly downhill, I'm afraid. At the end of the Fourth Dynasty, the dynasty of Sneferu, the dynasty of Khufu, we start to get some changes, and we're not sure exactly why.

The successor of Khufu, Djedefre, doesn't build a pyramid at Giza. For some reason he moves away to a place called Abu Roash several miles away, and he starts to build a strange kind of pyramid, building a big trench in the ground. He never finishes. We don't really know what it would have been. But after Djedefre, his successor comes back to Giza, and we start to get a sense that tradition is being restored. Now, the successor is Chephren. The Greeks called him Chephren, but the Egyptian name was really Khafre. It's the same person. Chephren builds a pyramid that is just about the same size as the Great Pyramid, only 20 feet smaller. You wonder why he built it a little bit smaller rather than a little bit bigger? Well, the answer is probably out of deference to his father, but it's a big pyramid.

He has an innovation, though, but it's accidental. He didn't plan it. It's the Sphinx. If you'll remember, when you built a pyramid in the Fourth Dynasty you didn't just build a pyramid, you had a complex. You had a mortuary temple next to it. There was a valley temple where perhaps you were mummified and a causeway connecting the valley temple to the pyramid. So once you were mummified in the valley temple your body would be brought in a sacred procession down this causeway and placed in the pyramid.

Well, if you trace the causeway from the pyramid of Chephren straight down to the valley temple, it's not a straight line. What happened was, they were excavating the causeway, digging through the sandstone, and they hit a huge rock, a sandstone rock. Rather than remove it, they carved the Sphinx out of it. The Sphinx is the head of a man (we're pretty sure it's Chephren) and the body of a lion. The idea is it symbolizes the intelligence of the man and the power of the lion. The lion is going to be a kind of pharaonic talisman, a totem animal. When Ramses the Great went into battle he had a pet lion with him. It would be pretty scary if you're going up against Ramses and he's got a lion next to him. So the Sphinx is really an accident. It wasn't planned.

Now, let me say a few things about the Sphinx. There are an awful lot of rumors about how old the Sphinx is. You've probably heard the controversy. Many people have started to say that the Sphinx is much older than believed. The Sphinx was constructed about 4,500 years ago, roughly, because it's Chephren who built it. We're virtually sure. But a couple of geologists have suggested, when they looked at the rock, that it looks like water erosion on the Sphinx. Now, if it's water erosion, there wasn't water there in 2500 B.C. or so. It's probably, they say, rain, that Egypt was much more moist at this point, and they pushed the date of the Sphinx back to 10,000 B.C. They are wrong. Let me just say it: They are wrong. Almost all Egyptologists agree the Sphinx was carved during the reign of Chephren.

One of the reasons we're quite sure that they are wrong is there was no significant Egyptian civilization in 10,000 B.C. that could have carved the Sphinx. Remember from our prehistoric lecture, they were just starting to learn about farming, even. So there is no doubt about it. The Sphinx is not from 10,000 B.C. It's more recent. It's still pretty impressive.

There are a couple of other myths about the Sphinx. One is that Napoleon, when he brought his expedition to Egypt in 1798, shot off the nose, that they were using the Sphinx for target practice. Now, there are two reasons why I can tell you that's false. One is Napoleon was really reverential to the ancient monuments. He had brought 150 scientists to study the monuments of Egypt. He wasn't about to blow them away. But the better, more convincing argument that Napoleon didn't shoot off the nose of the Sphinx is that we have drawings of the Sphinx done in the eighteenth century, earlier than when Napoleon was there, and the nose is missing then. The Sphinx's nose was missing probably for a thousand years. It's wind erosion that caused the nose to be gone.

Other myths about the Sphinx: Not all, but a lot of Freudian psychology is based on the idea that the Sphinx is a woman because of the hair. See, it looks like a woman's hair, but it's not a woman's hair. It's a cloth headdress that's called a *nemes* headdress that only the pharaoh wore. It's a kind of pleated thing. You see it on the gold mask of Tutankhamen, these striations going around. That's what the Sphinx is wearing. The Sphinx is not a woman. You know what is sort of funny about this headdress that the Sphinx wears? If you look at the really bad movies about Egypt, the grade "B" movies, you'll see that usually they've got the slaves and the servants wearing this headdress, but it was only for pharaohs. It was only for royalty.

There is another interesting thing about the Sphinx, and I can go on about the Sphinx forever. I love the Sphinx. The beard of the Sphinx—it's missing. Originally the Sphinx had a beard. Pharaohs wore false beards. Pharaohs were usually clean-shaven. Almost all the Egyptians were clean-shaven, but it was a sign of authority to have a beard. So they wore a little beard. It was probably plaited, made out of maybe straw or maybe even human hair, and had strings and a chin strap. For official occasions the pharaoh would tie on his beard. It would tie in the back. If you look at the Sphinx you will see that on the sides are indentations, which are indicating the chin strap. So we know that the Sphinx had a beard.

And now I'll tell you something that I'm sure you didn't know. I'll tell you where the beard is. It's in two places. One place surprised me. I didn't know it was there. Inside the Egyptian Museum in Cairo is a library called *Maktaba*. It's Arabic for "library." The librarian for many years was a wonderful old woman, Dr. Diablo Gazi. I went to visit her one day, and I almost fell on my head. I tripped over something. I asked her—I said, "Dr. Diablo, what did I trip on?" She said, "Oh, that's the beard of the Sphinx." There is a piece of the beard of the Sphinx that they found when excavating. It's probably three feet, four feet long, and it's just a piece of it. It's in the library on the floor in the Egyptian Museum in Cairo.

Now, there is another piece of the Sphinx's beard that exists in the British Museum, and that's a bit of a political problem. The Egyptian government would like to have the beard of the Sphinx back. Perhaps it can be restored. If you put the two pieces together maybe you've got something. Then you peg it in. You could put in a rod. It can be restored. Such things can be done nowadays. I think the British Museum would really like to give it back, but they can't. It's not on display, by the way, in the British Museum. It's simply in a basement storage area. But I think the problem is they don't want to start a precedent. If you give the beard of the Sphinx back to Egypt, the next thing they ask for is the Rosetta stone, so they are a little bit afraid of giving it back and saying, "Sure, why not? We don't need it." So the beard of the Sphinx exists in two places. One is the British Museum; the other is in the library at the Egyptian Museum in Cairo.

Now, when Chephren built his monument, he didn't expect to hit a big rock, so they just carved the Sphinx out. The causeway bends because they had to go around the Sphinx, so it's not a straight line, but it leads to the valley temple. This is where perhaps Chephren was mummified. The valley temple is a unique monument. It is the only large Egyptian temple we have from this period, and it shows us how they built them, out of huge stones. They are monoliths. They are large stones weighing maybe 20–30 tons, and it's the only thing we have of that kind. It has an alabaster floor, so it gives you an idea of the wealth they had to pave an entire temple with alabaster. Quite a few important statues were also found there, but that's Chephren. He was trying to continue the tradition. He was building a pyramid like the Great Pyramid. He was building a mortuary temple, a valley temple. He was keeping to tradition. But after him things change.

His successor is called Mycerinus by the Greeks—Menkaure in Egyptian. Mycerinus also built on the Giza Plateau, so you've got three fairly large pyramids on the Giza Plateau. You've got the Great Pyramid of Giza, which is Cheops/Khufu. You've got Chephren's, and now you have Mycerinus's, but it's smaller. It's about a fifth the size of the Great Pyramid. Why? It may be that the economy was changing. It may be that they were running out of money and didn't have the money to do it. But it's a little different kind of pyramid. It's small, as I said, but he tried to do something special, perhaps because it was small and he had to compensate. It's cased not with limestone—the outer casing isn't limestone. It's granite, pink Aswan granite—harder than limestone, more expensive, more lavish—but it's unfinished. If you look at the casing, you can see it's rounded on the ends. It would have been carved flat, flush with the pyramid, but it was never finished. That's the last of the pyramid building on the Giza Plateau.

What happens next? Something very strange. Mycerinus's successor is a pharaoh, the last pharaoh of his Dynasty, the last pharaoh of the Fourth Dynasty, the last of the family of Sneferu and Khufu, the

Great Pyramid builders, this family that grew up building pyramids. The last pharaoh is Shepseskaf. He moves away from Giza. Why? We don't know. There is still room on the Giza Plateau. There are a couple of other smaller pyramids on the Giza Plateau also. They are for queens, they are smaller, but there is room for other pyramids. But Shepseskaf says, "No." He moves back to Saqqara, back to where the Step Pyramid was built, where the pyramid building all started, and he doesn't build a pyramid. He builds a mastaba, going back, curious, breaking with tradition. It's called the *Mastabet el-Fara'oun* in Arabic. It means "the mastaba of the pharaoh," and it's in the shape of a cartouche—remarkable. But that's the end of the Fourth Dynasty. The Great Pyramid building era has ended. We're never going to see another pyramid like those of Sneferu, Khufu, Chephren. Never again. And, in a sense, Egypt will never return to this greatness.

The next dynasty is an interesting one, the Fifth Dynasty. There are big changes now, and we're not sure exactly why. Let me tell you about a papyrus. Remember I mentioned last time about the magical papyrus, called Papyrus Westcar, which told about Sneferu and how a maiden had lost an amulet? Well, this papyrus has lots of stories in it. It's in the Berlin Museum, and it tells a story of the beginning of Dynasty V.

The papyrus is set during the time of Khufu, builder of the Great Pyramid, and Khufu is having his sons—and there are plenty of them—tell him stories to amuse him. Each tells a story, and, when one son comes up, it's his turn, and he says, "Rather than telling a story, let me bring a magician, and he'll tell you the future." So a magician is brought in, and he starts to tell the future. What he sees is the beginning of the Fifth Dynasty. He says how the new dynasty is going to start, and he says it's going to start with the birth of triplets. These are going to be the first kings of the Fifth Dynasty. So we have this magical story about how the Fifth Dynasty begins.

We know that it begins with changes. The kings of the Fifth Dynasty—we can call them solar kings, sun kings—they seem to be really more into sun worship than anybody else. They innovate something that's never been seen in Egypt before, a solar temple, a temple dedicated to the sun. They have pyramids also—they are small affairs—but they go to different sites. They go to Abu Gurob and Abu Sir (these are about a mile apart from each other, not too far from Saqqara), and they built these sun temples. They are a large altar, and in front of the altar is a large stone. It's not quite an obelisk, but it's called a ben-ben stone. We don't really know the function. It was some kind of stone that was worshiped in some way. But they have these sun temples and small pyramids.

These pharaohs also have unusual names. The first one is Userkaf. That's not a strange name, but after him the pharaohs take "re" names, meaning, they incorporate "Re," the sun god, into their names. So we get people like Sahure, Neferikare. All of these are praising the sun god "Re." So they are building solar temples. They have names that incorporate "Re." Something is going on. I'm not sure exactly what. It could be that the priests are becoming sort of influential and saying, "You know, the right god is really "Re." He's the big god." So they are starting to change things, perhaps for religious reasons.

At the end of the Fifth Dynasty we get an even bigger change. The last king of the Fifth Dynasty starts a tradition that will be continued a little while, but it's absolutely unique. The Pharaoh Unas builds a pyramid at Saqqara. It's a small pyramid. It's modest, but inside it's incredible. He has texts carved inside all over the burial chamber, on the walls leading to the burial chamber, which we call the Pyramid Texts. Now, remember, up until this time one of the puzzles is, Why didn't they put names on the pyramids, even? Why are the burial chambers of, say, the Meidum Pyramid, the Red Pyramid, the Bent Pyramid, the Great Pyramids at Giza—why are they all blank walls, uninscribed? Nobody knows. But Unas changes this.

On the walls, covering the walls, are thousands of hieroglyphs, and they are all magical. They are called the Pyramid Texts, and what they are supposed to do is make sure that the pharaoh makes it to the next world. Now, people often say it's amazing that you can build the Great Pyramid of Cheops in 22 years, roughly the time it took to build it. I think it's amazing that Unas could build his pyramid because it took an incredible amount of work and labor, artists carving these hieroglyphs, and they go from ceiling to floor, in columns. Each column is a separate spell, hundreds of beautifully carved, painted hieroglyphs.

And, you know, I've looked at the hieroglyphs very carefully. I figured that the way to do it quickly, efficiently is to have stencils. Like when you were a kid and you wanted to do the ABCs nicely on your report, you could have a stencil, and you could do it, I figured they'd have hieroglyph stencils. So I looked very carefully at the owls, just that one hieroglyph, which is the hieroglyph for "M." The sound "M" is an owl. They were all individually done. They weren't stenciled on. You can tell. They are not the same. They are not all exactly the same height. The feathers don't go all the same way. These were each individual little sculptures, a remarkable thing. It would have taken years and years to do it. I often wondered, Did they do it on the wall, or did they do it outside and bring the blocks in? You know, you could have more men working. We're not sure. But it's a remarkable achievement.

Let me tell you what they say. The Pyramid Texts are intended to protect the body of the pharaoh in three different stages. Now, remember, the king is buried inside the pyramid, inside a sarcophagus, and the sarcophagus of Unas, by the way, is still there, and it's a thing of beauty. It's painted like the palace facade. Remember the *serekh*, that rectangle that represents a palace? It has paintings on it just like that, beautifully colored because there is no weathering inside the pyramid, so they still have the vibrant colors.

The first stage that the Pyramid Texts are supposed to take care of is to protect the body of the pharaoh as it lies in the burial chamber. So you get magical spells like, "Unas lies in his burial chamber. Nothing disturbs his rest. Unas is not bitten by a scorpion. No robber disturbs the rest of Unas." So the first spells are all to make sure that the body of the king will stay undisturbed in its sarcophagus until it's ready for the big journey.

The next stage is when the pharaoh is going to go across the sky to the west. Now, the west was always associated with the dead. Probably the reason is that the sun dies in the west every day and is reborn in the east. So, for example, during most of Egyptian civilization the Egyptians buried their dead on the west. They lived on the east bank but buried on the west. Almost all tombs are on the west bank. Pyramids are on the west. Almost always the west is the land of the dead. Even Osiris, the god of the dead, is called Lord of the West.

And you know what the Egyptians called people who died? We have euphemisms today. I mean, we don't say, "Oh, he's dead." If you go to a funeral, he might be "the dearly departed." It sounds like he just went on a trip. The Egyptians called them "westerners." Dead people were called "westerners," and when somebody died they said, "He went west." So the west was always associated with the dead. When you were going to make your journey to the next world, you were going to go through the sky to the west in a boat, a solar boat.

The next set of spells are intended to make sure that when Unas makes the big journey he's not going to be impeded in any way. The boat is going to have smooth sailing through the sky. So you have spells like, "The bark of Unas progresses swiftly. No enemy of Unas hinders the bark." You get things like that. So the second stage of the Pyramid Texts is to make sure that you're going to go west safely.

The third and last stage of the Pyramid Texts is that Unas is going to be accepted into the next world. He's made the journey. His body has been protected inside the sarcophagus in the burial chamber. It has stayed there until the time of resurrection, until he makes the big journey. Now we've got to make sure that he is accepted in the next world. So you have magical spells like, "Unas is greeted by Osiris. Unas is welcomed by Horus. Isis is on his left; Horus is on his right. They greet the pharaoh." So we're told that Unas makes it. It's a magical principle. The word is the deed. If you say it, it will happen.

There are a couple of spells that are kind of curious. First, about getting accepted into the next world, it's almost like they had backup systems. He's getting to the next world—how is he going to get in? "Unas ascends his ladder," and the gods are holding the ladder to steady it. So one way to get into the next world is by the ladder. Now, if that doesn't work, "Unas ascends the steps to the next world." Some people think that the steps may be the steps of a step pyramid. That may be what they intended to do. But Unas has plenty of ways to get into the next world, and that's the purpose of the Pyramid Texts.

There is one text that there has been a lot of literature about, a very strange text. It's called the Cannibal Hymn. It's on the walls of the pyramid, and we're pretty sure we know what it means. It describes Unas as eating the entrails of his enemy, and Unas eats parts of the gods, even. The notion, of course, is I guess that you've really defeated your enemy, and maybe even, if you eat his entrails or eat part of the gods, you gain their power. That's the notion. But the question is, Are we supposed to take this literally? Do we really want to think that Unas was a cannibal or that the Egyptians were cannibals? Well, most of us don't take it literally. We think the idea is, you know, it's like saying, "I'm going to knock your head off." You don't mean it literally.

But one Egyptologist did, and it led to a curious theory. E.A. Wallace Budge—he was the curator of the British Museum's Egyptian Collection. In those days, in the 1920s, he was called the Keeper of Egyptian Antiquities. Budge wrote a book on Osiris, and if you'll remember the myth, Budge has an explanation for this myth. Osiris, if you remember, is the first one to resurrect. He's hacked to pieces, he's put back together, and he resurrects. So the Egyptian religion is one of resurrection. Budge claims that this myth was introduced to stop the Egyptians from being cannibals. See, if you told them, "No, no. Don't eat that relative. He needs his body for the next world," then it would stop cannibalism.

So Budge at least is one who took this myth literally as true. Most of us think he's wrong, that it wasn't literally true. There is virtually no evidence for cannibalism in Egyptian society. There are no bones, for example, with human teeth marks on it, which is how you would tell. There are no texts that say anything like that. So almost certainly it's merely metaphorically, and Unas is going to make it to the next world.

Unas is the last king of Dynasty V. The kings of Dynasty VI are going to build pyramids at Saqqara, but they are small things, really inconsequential. If you look at them today they look very much like hills. They look almost like natural hills. You can't really tell they were once beautiful pyramids. Now, the Pharaoh Teti in Dynasty VI built a pyramid, as I said, a small affair, nothing impressive. But at the same time that he was building his little pyramid, which included Pyramid Texts, his chancellor Mereruka is building his mastaba. Now, remember, the mastabas are the above ground benchlike structures. Mereruka's mastaba is so big that it rivals the pyramid of the pharaoh.

What I think we're getting is the pharaoh's power is being diminished and the nobles around him are increasing in wealth. We don't know why. But if you look at Mereruka's mastaba it has 32 rooms. It's practically an apartment house, and all the rooms are carved with beautiful scenes of what Mereruka wanted to do in the next world. It shows him harpooning a hippo—he was a hunter. It shows fishing scenes. It shows him with his family banqueting. It's 32 rooms of beauty. It must have taken an incredible amount of manpower to do something like that. And inside Mereruka's little chamber is a beautiful statue. It's beautiful. It rivals royal art. It shows Mereruka, and he's standing in a kilt.

Now, let me tell you something about this kilt. This kilt was a sign. It's a starched kilt. It was worn by officials, and what that means is, I'm an official. I've got this starched kilt. I couldn't possibly do manual labor. It's like the Mandarin fingernails that were a sign that the Mandarins didn't have to do any work. This was a way of saying, I'm an official. I don't have to do anything. So Mereruka built this incredible mastaba while the pyramid of the pharaoh isn't really anything special. I think we're really getting almost a competition between the pharaoh and his nobility.

Let me say a couple of things about the last pharaoh of Dynasty VI. This is going to be the end of the Old Kingdom. I use the words "Old Kingdom." Egyptian history is so long, 3,200 years virtually of recorded history, of records that we have, that you have to break it up into manageable chunks or it all just becomes too much. Egyptologist do that in a simple way. The beginning we call the Old Kingdom. At the end of the Old Kingdom there was a total collapse. That's an intermediate period: First Intermediate Period. Then Egypt rises again and gets its act together. We call that the Middle Kingdom—years of prosperity, stability—but then it collapses again. As far as I know, Egypt is the only civilization to have two really total collapses and get its act together again, the only one.

Then, when it gets its act together again, we call it the New Kingdom. So we've got Old Kingdom, Intermediate Period, Middle Kingdom, Intermediate Period, New Kingdom, and then there is going to be Late Period and Decline. This is Egyptology talk. The Egyptians never talked that way. They never said, "We're in the New Kingdom now." They never viewed it that way, but we view it that way. So what we're looking at right now in Dynasty VI is the end of the Old Kingdom. It's the end of the glory days.

The last pharaoh of Dynasty VI, who ends the Old Kingdom, is a pharaoh called Pepi II. He has a couple of distinctions that are kind of neat. Pepi II is the longest-reigning monarch in the history of the world. He ruled for 94 years—94 years. Of course he was a child when he ascended to the throne, maybe only four years old, but that means he lived to be 98—the longest reigning monarch in the history of the world.

There is even a great story connected with him when he was a kid, when he was a kid pharaoh. He's eight years old, and he's got his chancellor to Nubia in the south. He sent him to Nubia to bring back gold and ivory and all these great things, of course, or at least somebody sent him—Pepi's only eight years old. The chancellor writes back and says, "I'm also bringing you a pigmy," and Pepi gets so excited. He writes back to his chancellor. He says, "I want this pigmy more than the gold." He says, "Put strong men on either side of him when he goes to the river so he doesn't fall in and drown. Have strong men sleeping next to him in his tent, but I want this pigmy. I will reward you more than anyone." And the pigmy makes it back. And this letter that Pepi II as a kid wrote to his chancellor in Nubia, the chancellor, on his tomb, put it on the wall. He had it carved on the wall, showing that the pharaoh cared enough to write a personal letter. It was a big deal. So we've got a little bit of documentation on Pepi II as a kid.

But he lives very long, maybe too long. Remember, the pharaoh was the physical leader of Egypt. He had to take the men out in the army. He had to do battle. He had to lead. Pepi lives to be perhaps 98. That may be the reason why the Old Kingdom collapsed. Pepi may have just lived too long. He could no longer lead the army. He was feeble. What could you do? He's a god-king—he stays put. This may be the reason why the Old Kingdom eventually collapsed with Pepi II. That's the danger of having a pharaoh-centric government, all the power in the hands of one person. If he's great he can do great things. But if he's not great you could be in trouble. It may have led to the First Intermediate Period, the total collapse of Egyptian civilization, and we'll talk about that next time.

Lecture Eleven
The First Intermediate Period (2181–2040 B.C.)

Scope:

Here we will see trouble in paradise. After centuries of powerful growth, the rise of nationhood, pyramids, and prosperity, Egypt totally collapses. We will explore the possible causes of this collapse but, more important, we will examine the consequences for religion, art, and politics of this anarchy that descended on Egypt. We will also use the First Intermediate Period to show the methods Egyptologists use to reconstruct history when the historical sources are scant.

Outline

I. Physicist Kurt Mendelssohn's theory was that Egypt declined because unemployed laborers revolted against the pharaonic order—he was probably wrong. In reconstructing the First Intermediate Period, we use various sources. One of them is Manetho (third century B.C.), an Egyptian priest who wrote a history of Egypt (*Aegyptiaka*) in Greek for Ptolemy II.

   A. The original text of Manetho is lost, but we have quotations from later ancient sources: "70 kings in 70 Days." In other words, there was no stability.

   B. Another possibility is that there may have been simultaneous kings in the north and south. We do know the capital changed during this period—from Memphis to Herakleopolis.

II. Kings lists are a basic historical resource of ancient Egypt. Carved on temple walls or written on papyrus, they list the chain of pharaohs.

   A. The Palermo Stone goes up to Dynasty V. Our oldest record, it gives the years of reigns and some details but ends before the First Intermediate Period.

   B. The Karnak List, today in the Louvre, has 61 kings up to Tuthmosis III.

C. The Abydos List, with 76 kings up to Seti I, was used in rituals. Once a year, the pharaoh would read the names of kings in the Hall of the Ancients in order to provision them in the next world.

D. The Turin Papyrus originally listed 300 kings up to Ramses II, with some details of their reigns. The papyrus is badly damaged.

III. The literature of the Middle Kingdom, which looks back to the intermediate period, also yields information. Of special importance are lamentations, a type of literature used as a source of history.

A. One lamentation concerns a man about to commit suicide. His *ba* (personality) threatens to desert him if he does, which means the man wouldn't be able to resurrect.

B. The lamentations reveal that Egypt was invaded by foreigners. A major theme of the lamentations is that divine order is upset, contrary to the tradition Egypt so long revered. Who was responsible for maintaining divine order? The pharaoh.

C. This *maat* (divine order) resembled the Elizabethan Great Chain of Being—the world was structured according to God's plan.

D. The lamentations are nostalgic about the good old days of Sneferu. The social order was being trampled—this was the period when the great pyramids were robbed.

E. The lamentations reflect the Egyptians' fear of the desert and the Bedouins who populate it. For Egyptians, their well-watered land was the best place on earth.

F. Finally, the lamentations even question the taxing of people in difficult times. Egypt was the largest bureaucracy in the history of the world, and its government was supported by taxing the peasants according to how high the Nile rose.

IV. We know little about the First Intermediate Period.

A. Dynasties VII and VIII (2181–2160 B.C.) ruled from Memphis.

B. Excavations at Memphis are difficult because of the high water table and extensive cultivation, and thus it's a "lost city." Because the capital is gone, the First Intermediate Period is hard to study. But Egypt, as we shall see, will rise again.

Essential Reading:

Aidan Dodson, *Monarchs of the Nile*, Chapter V.

Supplementary Reading:

Peter Clayton, *Chronicle of the Pharaohs*, pp. 60–68.

Questions to Consider:

1. What are our sources of information for this obscure period?
2. What was life like for the nobility during this period?

Lecture Eleven—Transcript
The First Intermediate Period (2181–2040 B.C.)

Hello again. Remember last time I was telling you about the changes at the end of the Old Kingdom? Well, for Egypt change is always bad. It always leads to something bad. It's going to lead to the First Intermediate Period. But let me review the changes that we saw. The last king of Dynasty IV didn't even build a pyramid. Shepseskaf, remember, builds the Mastaba el-Faraoun in the desert, and then with the Fifth Dynasty we get kings changing their names to have "ra" at the end or "re," solar gods. They build temples rather than big pyramids. They are building solar temples.

There are all kind of changes. The last king of Dynasty V starts putting Pyramid Texts on the walls. I think the priests are controlling things. Anyway, at the end we saw Dynasty VI, the last dynasty of the Old Kingdom, end with Pepi II, the longest-reigning monarch in the history of the world, ruling for 94 years, and the suggestion was that maybe he just got too old. Maybe he just couldn't lead that army in battle anymore. Maybe he couldn't control the government anymore, and Egypt just declined.

There is another theory. I should be fair to Kurt Mendelssohn. There is another theory about why Egypt took a nosedive. Now, Kurt Mendelssohn is not an Egyptologist. He's a physicist (he's dead now) who had a theory about the pyramids and pyramid building, and his book—it's a wonderful book—is called *The Riddle of the Pyramids*. It's one of those great books and rare books that are mostly wrong but still worth reading. He didn't get it right, but he is an intelligent man thinking through things. He had a theory about why there was a decline. Remember after the Fourth Dynasty, after those great pyramids of Sneferu and Cheops and Chephren, there were no longer any big pyramids built? His idea is that that's why the government declined.

What happened was you had 90,000 guys working on a pyramid, and all of a sudden maybe the priests convinced the pharaohs not to build big pyramids anymore. What do you have? Unemployed laborers. And maybe you have this large workforce no longer employed: They revolt and cause problems, and maybe that's the reason for the decline. That was Mendelssohn's theory. I don't think it's right. I think most of the laborers were farmers who were free during inundation, and they went back to their farms. But I just wanted to be fair and give you another theory.

So, in any event, the Old Kingdom ends with a lot of changes and a decline. Then comes the First Intermediate Period. It's a period about which we know hardly anything. It lasts for as long as the United States has been a country. Nearly 200 years it lasts, and we hardly know anything. It's a curious thing that you could have a Dark Age for so long, but that's how long Egyptian history is. Now, how do you reconstruct history when you don't have any records? There are practically no records of this period. It's a problem because, remember, it's the government that kept the records in ancient Egypt. Private people didn't keep records. Private people couldn't write, most of them.

Well, we use various sources, and I'm going to tell you today about the First Intermediate Period, about what happened, what we think happened, but I'm also going to use it to try to show you how Egyptologists piece together a picture of a period that we don't know much about. One source is Manetho. He's a priest. He's an Egyptian priest who was alive at the time of the Ptolemies. These are the Greeks who ruled Egypt at the very end of the civilization. Manetho was alive in the third century B.C., and he wrote a history of Egypt called *Aegyptiaka*, "About Egypt."

Now, the virtue that Manetho has is he's an Egyptian priest. He's an insider. He had access to temple records. He could read the hieroglyphs. So he's going to write a history of Egypt, but it's called *Aegyptiaka*. That's Greek. Why is he writing in Greek? Well, the answer is that Egypt is being controlled by Greeks. He is writing for his king, who's a Greek. So he writes a history of Egypt in Greek so that the pharaoh, Ptolemy II, can read it and he can read about the glorious history of Egypt.

What does Manetho, our source, say about this First Intermediate Period? What does he say about it? Well, first of all, we don't have the original text of Manetho. His original work is lost, but he's quoted all the time by later historians, guys like Eusebius and Africanus, and we have their quotes. What did Manetho say? He says, of the First Intermediate Period, "There were 70 kings in 70 days." What does he mean? Now, first of all, I'm pretty sure he didn't mean it literally. It's a very high turnover of pharaohs.

What he probably means is that there were many pharaohs who didn't reign very long, that these were kings who didn't last. That's one possibility. Almost always in Egyptian civilization, when you get kings with short reigns, coming one after the other, it's a sign that there is something wrong. Stability is when you get a king reigning for 20 years, another 20 years, 10, 15 years. When you get short reigns there is a problem. So Manetho says "70 kings in 70 days"— maybe short reigns.

I'll give you another possibility. There may have been simultaneous kings. For example, as you remember, the capital is Memphis in the north. You may have had people in the north claiming to be king. That could be. Then in the south you may have other people who are kind of ruling in the south, saying, I'm king. So you may even get simultaneous kings. So there are a lot of possibilities here, a lot of possibilities. One thing we know about the First Intermediate Period is the capital changed. See, Dynasties VII and VIII are in the First Intermediate Period. They are in Memphis. But then the capital moves south to a place called Herakleopolis.

Herakleopolis is the name that the Greeks called it. They associate it with their god Herakles, so it's "Herakles's City." But in ancient Egyptian times during the First Intermediate Period there was a god there called Herishef, who was a ram-headed god. And we know the capital moved from Memphis to the south, Herakleopolis. That suggests something big happened. Either the kings couldn't rule anymore in Memphis, or there is a takeover, or the priests have said, the gods are more important here. It's a big deal to move a capital. Think about moving our capital from Washington, D.C. Egypt had a big bureaucracy, believe me, and it wasn't an easy thing. The records were in Memphis. The scribes were in Memphis. It was a big deal. So there may have been kings all over the place. We just don't know. But Manetho is a key source. Seventy kings in 70 days—that's all we know.

What other sources do we have? Well, one of the prime sources when we're trying to figure out which kings ruled when, are the kings' lists. The pharaohs were very proud of their continued lineage. They loved to trace their heritage back from him to him to him to him. It's like the "begets" in the Bible, and it's like people today tracing back their lineage to the Mayflower. Genealogy is big now; it was big then.

The kings' lists were carved on temple walls often or even just on stones, sometimes written on papyrus, listing all the previous kings. So as soon as you became king you started writing, "I'm now, and before me was so and so," and you trace it back as much as you can. We have lots of these kings' lists. One is called the Palermo Stone. It's fragments. It's just pieces, but it's a long, dark stone that has carved on it the reigns of pharaohs and even things that happened during their reigns. So it's an important source for us. But the problem with the Palermo Stone is the First Intermediate Period begins with Dynasty VII, the Palermo Stone goes up to Dynasty V— it's not going to help us. It's a real early monument, so that won't work. Another kings' list, the Karnak List, as it's called, was once carved on Karnak Temple, which is in Thebes, south, and it has 61 kings up to the time of the Pharaoh Tuthmose III, but it doesn't tell us anything about the First Intermediate Period. It doesn't help.

Now, there is another one. Maybe one of the best is the Abydos Kings' List. Abydos, remember, is the sacred city where Osiris was eventually buried, where the early kings had their burials, and a later pharaoh, Seti I, built his temple at Abydos. On the wall inside one of the rooms he created what he called the "Hall of the Ancients." It was his genealogy table listing the kings from Narmer to Seti I, and it wasn't just a list. No, this was used in a ritual. Once a year the pharaoh would come into this Hall of the Ancients, and he would look at this list of kings' names, and he would start to read them.

Now, why is he reading the names of the kings? Well, above the kings' names is a prayer, and the prayer says, "May the king grant a wish to Anubis," and it's a funerary prayer, and it says, "May the god give bread and beer, food, cattle, geese and oxen, all things good and pure upon which the god lives, may he give all these things to these kings." So by reading the names of these kings they are going to get food, bread, beer, clothing, alabaster, linen, everything needed in the next world. So a kings' list is important, but it doesn't help us with the First Intermediate Period. We still really don't know.

The one that would have helped us most is the Turin Papyrus. It listed originally 300 kings. We can tell by its length. But it was written on papyrus, and the papyrus is badly damaged, and we just really can't reconstruct the First Intermediate Period from there. It's a problem. So the kings' lists don't help us much; Manetho—"70 kings in 70 days." What do you do? Well, you turn to literature.

There is fiction, although not written right during the First Intermediate Period. As I said, we hardly have any literature from that time. What we do is we go to fiction written during the next period, called the Middle Kingdom, just after, and there is a body of literature called "Lamentations." It's where people are complaining— it's lamenting. It's a large genre. There are plenty of papyri to talk about this. And it gives us an insight into what was going on in this First Intermediate Period.

I'm going to read a little bit to you of "Lamentations," but let me tell you first about my favorite example of a lamentation. There is a papyrus that's called "The Report of a Dispute between a Man and His Ba." The Egyptians believed that a person was made up of many parts. The physical body is part of it, but there was also a soul. The soul had lots of different parts, aspects. One was called the *ka*. That's sort of like a physical double, and you could have a *ka* statue, even. In case your mummy was destroyed, you would have at least something that looked like you. That's the *ka*. But probably the most important part was the *ba*. The *ba* was your personality. It's what makes you you. They used to represent the *ba* in a kind of curious way. You will see it drawn on tomb walls and in papyri, in Books of the Dead. It's got the head of a man, the deceased, and the body of a bird, and the idea is that this *ba* could kind of flit in and out of the tomb until it was time to resurrect. There were other parts, too, but the important parts are the body, the *ka*, and the *ba*.

Now, this papyrus, "The Report of a Dispute between a Man and His Ba," talks about a man who is about to commit suicide. He's really unhappy. It's probably the First Intermediate Period, and he laments, he says, "There is no justice in the world. Things are terrible." He says, "I have no one to talk to, and brothers kill each other." All kinds of horrible things he describes, and he says, "I'm going to kill myself." The *ba* steps in and talks to him. That's why it's a report of a dispute between a man and his *ba*. The *ba* says, "Huh uh, don't kill yourself. It's wrong."

It's interesting—it's a kind of philosophical discussion. Is suicide justified? And the man says, "I'll tell you what I'll do, *ba*. I'm going to kill myself," and the *ba* says, "I'll tell you what happens. If you kill yourself, I'm going to desert you. You're not going to have me in the west in the next world, and then you can't resurrect." And the man says to the *ba*—he's talking to his soul—he's says, "Listen, I will make for you a tomb that will make every *ba* envious of you. You're going to have the best tomb ever. Just don't desert me." And the *ba* says, "No. If you kill yourself, you're out of immortality."

Now, the papyrus ends. It breaks off. It's damaged. We don't know what happens in the end. But at least we've got a guy lamenting, complaining, thinking about suicide, and the *ba* says, "It's wrong. Don't do it. I'll desert you." That's a lament. It's my favorite because it's kind of personalized, but there are more. It's a whole genre, and let me give you an idea of the kinds of things that people were saying in these lamentations. It's kind of neat, and you'll see.

Here is a lament that's written in the Middle Kingdom, but you'll see it's got some funny things in it. This is somebody complaining. He's talking about the First Intermediate Period, how bad things were, and he says, "Foreign bowmen [meaning bow and arrow] have come into Egypt." Now, think about it. For the first time since the unification of Egypt, since Narmer, Egypt is invaded. Bowmen—that's sort of a negative, negative, negative way to describe foreigners. Who would have ever thought that soon after the building of the Great Pyramid that Egypt would be invaded, that there are foreigners roaming. Then it says something much more sort of telltale. It says, "Lo—gold, lapis lazuli, silver, turquoise, carnelian, strung around the necks of slave girls."

Now, what's wrong with slave girls having lapis and carnelian, nice things? The answer is, divine order is upset. It's turned upside down. See, the Egyptians were the most conservative of all people. They didn't want change. That's why I stressed in the Fifth Dynasty that there is change. That's bad. The Egyptians never wanted change. They were the most conservative people in the world. It's kind of the original, "If it's not broke, don't fix it." Egypt was on top of the world. Why would you want change?

They believed that there was a divine order that the gods established, and that meant Egypt was at the top, ruling the Middle East. It also meant that lords had good things and slaves had not much. That was the way it was supposed to be. Now, who was responsible for making sure that divine order is established and stays put? The pharaoh. By making offerings to the gods, by going into the temples, the pharaoh would make sure that the gods were pleased, and then divine order would remain.

It's a little bit like a business deal. Most religion is in a sense like a business deal. I mean, what is a priest? It's somebody who intercedes for you to the gods. He's a businessman carrying out the transaction, and that's what the pharaoh was. He was carrying out the transaction of making sure that his country was getting its fair share. So when the pharaoh went into battle he would come back with lots of booty, and he would give a share to the temple, and then the temples would look on Egypt, and divine order would be restored.

But we've got slave girls wearing lapis. That's not right. That's not right. Everything had its place. You know what it's a little bit like? In Elizabethan times, during the time of Shakespeare, there was the belief in the great chain of being, that everything had its place, and they drew up these long diagrams of how the world was structured according to God's plan. At the top, of course, is God. Beneath God are angels. There are seraphim and cherubim. These are orders of angels. Beneath the angels you've got man, and of course there is a hierarchy there. At the top you've got the king and beneath him the lords and beneath them the peasants. It goes all the way down. Beneath man you've got the plants and animals.

There is a king of the animal world, the lion, and you've got lions going down, and then you've got the plants. Now, I don't know what the king of the plants is. Maybe it's broccoli. I don't know. But then beneath the plants (they are live plants), you've got the minerals, the lowest of the low, the insensitive things. So there was a sense of everything in its place. There was an order, a divine order, and that's exactly what the Egyptians believed in, divine order. They called it *maat*. Maat was a goddess, but also she represented truth, justice, and order. She's often shown, by the way, with a feather on top of her head. That's the hieroglyph for "true." It means truth, also justice. So there was this divine order, and that's what they were upset about. Divine order was turned upside down.

Let me give you another example. In this lamentation, continuing, he says, "None, indeed, sail north to Byblos today. What shall we do for pine trees for our mummies?" Now, what does that mean? Well, what it means is he wants the great old days of Sneferu, when Sneferu sent out expeditions to Lebanon, to Byblos. That's what he is looking for. He's looking for the good old days. Now, why do you need pines for mummies? The answer is, pine trees were the source of resin, and in order to make a good mummy you needed resin.

After you dehydrated it, you covered the face with tree sap to kind of seal it in, and resin was the way you stuck it together. The mummies were wrapped in bandages, but they didn't have regular glue. They used tree resin.

So when he says, "None, indeed, sail north to Byblos today," he's really saying, it's not like the good old days of Sneferu, and that's what he wanted, the good old days of Sneferu. So things are really bad and he says, this lamentation, what shall we do about it? All is in ruin. I mean, things are really bad. He says, "Lo, every have-not is one who has." That's just the wrong thing. There is no more sense that you should give to the poor or anything like that. The poor are supposed to be poor. That's what they are there for.

And he's got loads of interesting little tidbits. He says, "Lo, those who are entombed are cast on high ground." What he means is that people are robbing the tombs. They are robbing tombs, taking the bodies out, and casting them up. Remember, tombs are down in the ground, and people are going into the tombs, taking the bodies, and throwing them out.

To this day there is a parallel to that in Egypt. The ancient Egyptian word for cemetery was often "the city of the dead." They called it that, "houses of the dead," and today in Egypt there is a "City of the Dead." It's the modern cemetery in Cairo, and housing is so bad in Cairo that there are something like half a million people living in the tombs in the cemetery in Cairo called the "City of the Dead," and it's acknowledged by the government, even, because they have run in electricity for these people. So they just live in the tombs. So some things never change.

But he goes on. He talks about this inversion of wealth. He says, "Wearers of fine linen are beaten with sticks"—not very good—and he continues. He says, "Ladies suffer like maidservants." The idea is that maidservants are supposed to suffer. That's their place in life. And he says, "Lo, all maidservants are rude in their speech when the mistress speaks. It irks the servants." Things are bad.

Now, this is just one example of lamentations. There is another one that is called the "Prophecies of Neferti," and it's supposed to take place in the time of Sneferu. Now, remember, Sneferu is my hero. He's the one who shows Egypt how to build the pyramids, but he's also the guy that they all look back to as the great days. I'll tell you, a thousand years after Sneferu was dead, a thousand years after Sneferu was dead, when a pharaoh did something great, they said, not since the time of Sneferu has its like been done. So Sneferu was kind of like the good old days. And there are prophecies that supposedly take place in the time of Sneferu. Somebody is going to make predictions for Sneferu of what's going to happen, and he predicts the First Intermediate Period. Now, it's not a real prophecy. It's written during the Middle Kingdom—it's looking back—but it's got some wild stuff.

He says, "Lo, the great no longer rule the land. What was made has been unmade." They had tradition. "What is made has been unmade." What's been unmade? The pyramids. They have been robbed. During this First Intermediate Period, there were no bodyguards. There was no police state. There was nothing. It was anarchy. So the pyramids are big, hulking targets, and that's when the pyramids of Egypt are robbed. That's why we never find a body in the pyramid. They were all robbed during the First Intermediate Period. And this man is lamenting. He says, "Lo, the great no longer rule the land," meaning people like Sneferu. You're going to get a theme throughout all the lamentations. It's, first, divine order is upset, and, second, we need a champion. We need the king to come out on his horse and ride in with his hat and save us. That's what Egypt always turned towards, a champion, somebody to save them.

A couple more things. It's deeper than political problems they felt. It was, the gods are angry or something. He says, "Dry is the river of Egypt. One crosses it on foot." That's something very elemental. Even nature is against Egypt. Things have turned against Egypt, and they don't know why. He continues—there is more—he says, "The land is bowed down in distress owing to those feeders [Asiatics], who roam the land." Again, there is something wrong. Foreigners are entering into Egypt. Remember, Sneferu is the one who called himself the smiter of barbarians. He's the one who went into the Sinai. Things are bad.

And he says, "Desert flocks will drink at the river of Egypt." Now, what does that mean? "Desert flocks will drink at the river of Egypt." What's wrong with that? The answer is that the desert flocks are the Bedouins, the people of the desert. You see, it's a common misconception that the Egyptians were desert folk, riding into the desert on their camels. Egyptians hated the desert, feared it. They didn't have the camel until much later, until the Romans introduced it. The Egyptians stayed away from the desert. Everybody in Egypt lived along the Nile where the water was. So the desert was feared, and the people of the desert were to be kept at arm's length. Keep them out. So now he says, "Desert flocks will drink at the river of Egypt, take their ease on the shores for lack of one to fear." In other words, in the good old days those Bedouins were afraid to come near our river. They had to look for wells and stay away. But now they come and take their ease. Things are really bad.

See, Egypt was interesting towards foreigners. They didn't really like foreigners in the beginning. Egypt was the place you wanted to be. It was the place where you had to be buried. It was the place where you lived. It was the best place on earth. When an Egyptian went to a foreign country and it rained—the Egyptians never saw rain, hardly ever saw rain—they said, "It's curious. They have their Nile in the sky." And they viewed it as really unfortunate. You know why? They had to just wait for it to come. I mean, like nowadays, sometimes there is a drought, and sometimes it rains too much. But the Nile at least was always there. So Egypt was the best place on earth, and during this First Intermediate Period it had ceased to be the best place on earth. Why? They must have wondered. They just didn't know.

I'll give you one last goody or two of these lamentations. I love "Lamentations" because it gives you an insight to what these people felt about the land. He says, "The land is ruined, its fate decreed"— decreed by the gods, right? Deprived of produce, lacking crops. Everything is gone. "I show you the master's need." The master needs something? Incredible, never would happen. He says, "The land is shrunk. Its rulers are many. It is bare, but taxes are great." So people are not producing—the Nile is perhaps dry—and they are still being taxed. Something is really wrong. Taxes were almost a symbol of Egypt.

Ancient Egypt is probably the first country that really taxes its people systematically. Egypt was the largest bureaucracy in the history of the world. Think about it. If you've got a strong central government, you've got an army. You've got to pay that army. How do you get the money, the goods to pay the army? Egypt didn't have any currency. There was no currency in Egypt. They did barter. It was grain for clothes and this and that. Well, the way you paid the army and the priests and the people who didn't contribute to the society is you taxed the peasants. And how did you tax them? You didn't go and say, give me one-fifth of your grain. No, because they could cheat. They could hide the grain. They could say, "We had a bad year."

The peasants were taxed by how high the Nile rose. There were "Nilometers," measurements of the Nile carved on boulders in the river, and depending on how high the Nile rose that's how you were taxed. If the Nile rises, say, up to 22 feet, you're taxed this amount. You should be able to grow this amount of crops if the Nile is this high. If you grow that much you pay it. If you say you had a bad year, you still have to pay that amount. It doesn't matter. You can't hide your grain. If you're lucky and you grow more, you just have to pay that amount, but you're taxed not on how much you grow but how much you should be able to grow with the Nile of a certain height. So this man is saying, "There are no crops and the taxes are great." Things are really bad.

And he says, "One salutes he who was saluted." In other words, you're saluting the wrong guys. It's saluting the guy who should be saluting you. Then at the end he says, "Men will live in a graveyard. A beggar will gain riches. The slave will be exalted." Things are terrible. Divine order is upset.

Now, it's from texts like these—which is literature, it can't be taken perfectly literally—that we get an insight into what's going on in the First Intermediate Period for 200 years. Why do we have to go to texts like these? Well, one thing is that we don't have the official records. Another is that Manetho, our good source, is very scant: "70 kings in 70 days." And there is another reason: the kings' lists didn't help us much. But the other reason is that, in the beginning of this First Intermediate Period, the capital was at Memphis in the north, and Memphis is a lost city. The water table is higher in Memphis, and that means that buildings sink down. It means the papyrus on which records are written rots in the moisture.

If you try to excavate at Memphis, it's very difficult. You dig down three feet, and you're in water. It was excavated by Flinders Petrie, my man. They excavated in the nineteenth century, and he went around with an iron rod poking in to feel where the stones were under the mud and then tried to get the mud out, dig up a stone, but most of Memphis is under the mud. It's gone. It's a lost city. So when I tell you the history of Egypt I'm really not telling you, in a sense, the history of Egypt from the north. What we know is the history of Egypt from the south, where it was always dry and we have more records. It's kind of like looking under the lamppost for your watch—even though you didn't lose it there—because the light is there. All we have, really, are southern records. So another reason why the First Intermediate Period is so, so difficult to study is that the capital of Memphis is gone.

Now, there is good news. For nearly 200 years Egypt was in this period of anarchy. The good news is it rises again. It comes out of the mire. We're going to get the champion that they want to unify Egypt, but that's for next time. I'll see you then.

Lecture Twelve
The Middle Kingdom: Dynasty XI (2134–1991 B.C.)

Scope:

At the end of the Old Kingdom, the unthinkable happened: Egypt collapsed and was thrown into anarchy. The Middle Kingdom is the story of the resurrection of Egypt.

It is made up of only two dynasties: XI and XII. First we will look at Dynasty XI, the dynasty of unification. We will see Egypt slowly come under a single strong ruler once again and rise to greatness. We will also see that the names of the kings often provide clues to the political state of the country.

Outline

I. Dynasty XI (2134–1991 B.C.) began with kings all named Intef, so the chronology is a bit confusing. They were more Theban princes than true kings.

    A. The Intefs, residing in the south, tried for unification. Intef Seher-towi (2134–2117 B.C.) begins the dynasty. His name means "makes peace in the two lands," and he wrote his name in a cartouche. He had aspirations, but isn't really king of the two lands.

    B. Intef Wahankh (2117–2069 B.C.), "established in life," was a dog lover, the first in history. An Egyptologist found a stela in 1860 showing his five dogs. (Egyptians were lovers of both cats and dogs.) This pharaoh called himself "King of Upper and Lower Egypt."

    C. Intef Nakht-neb-tep-nefer (2069–2060 B.C.), "beautiful and strong champion," fought with northern rulers, trying to unify Egypt.

II. The Intefs are followed by the Montuhoteps ("the war god is pleased").

    A. Montuhotep I (also called Montuhotep II), Se-Ankh-ib-towi (2060–2010 B.C.), "He Gives Life to the Heart of the Two Lands," is the new political hope. Later, he added to his Horus name Sam-towi, "Uniter of the Two Lands," a sign of his accomplishment in unifying the two lands. He took the name Neb-Hepet-Re ("Pleased is the Lord Re") as his prenomen.

B. A warrior king who really was the unifier, Montuhotep left records of his battles up and down the Nile.

   1. He built a spectacular mortuary temple in Thebes that has been excavated several times.

   2. In the late nineteenth century, Swiss Egyptologist Edouard Naville found three princesses buried there, poorly mummified.

   3. In the 1920s, American archaeologist Herbert Winlock found two more princesses, one only five years old but a "lady of the harem"—a daughter of the court, a 'palace kid.'

   4. In Middle Kingdom burials, people are placed on their sides so they can look out of the coffin through two eyes painted on it. Often the insides of the coffins are inscribed with spells to help the deceased get to the next world.

   5. In the 1920s, Winlock found a mass burial at Thebes of over sixty mummies in Deir el Bahri, or "place of the northern monastery" in Arabic. The mummies all turned out to be young men—a group of soldiers brought back for burial.

   6. Winlock made further discoveries in a previously excavated tomb. The tomb of Meket re, chancellor and steward of the palace of Montuhotep I, contained remarkable wooden tomb models, like dioramas, depicting such amenities as bakeries and breweries that he expected to find in the next world.

   7. In another tomb, Winlock also found the silver scarab, or beetle, worn by Wah, a man who worked for Meket re. The eyes of the scarab were hacked out so it wouldn't be able to bite the deceased.

   8. Winlock also found the family letters of a Ka priest, Heka Nakht, that revealed him to be a querulous micromanager of the family estate. Agatha Christie based her novel *Death Comes as the End* on these letters.

C. Montuhotep Se-Ankh-Ka-Re (2010–1998 B.C.), "Causing the soul (ka) of Re to live," succeeded his father. He sent 3,000 men to the caravan route of the Wadi Hammamat in year 8 and was reported to have dug twelve wells along the way.

D. Montuhotep Neb-towi-Re (1997–1991 B.C.) followed, though few records exist of his reign. He sent 10,000 men under his Vizier Amenemhet to the Wadi Hammamat for stone. A pregnant gazelle led them to the stone to be used and gave birth on it. They sacrificed the gazelle.

E. This was a dynasty that could build big and mount large expeditions—this was Egypt reborn.

Essential Reading:

H. E. Winlock, *The Rise and Fall of the Middle Kingdom in Thebes.*

Supplementary Reading:

Aidan Dodson, *Monarchs of the Nile*, Chapter VI.

Questions to Consider:

1. How did Egypt eventually become a nation again?

2. What were the accomplishments of the pharaohs who unified Egypt?

Lecture Twelve—Transcript
The Middle Kingdom—Dynasty XI

Welcome back. Let me do a little bit of recapping just for a minute or two about where we left off last time. If you'll remember, Egyptian civilization had totally collapsed. We were in what we called the First Intermediate Period. Perhaps it was caused by the last king of the Old Kingdom, Pepi II, who reigned for 94 years. Perhaps he just reigned too long and couldn't control the army, and maybe Egypt just sort of slid downhill.

Whatever the cause, the political system collapsed. There was virtually total anarchy in Egypt. We have perhaps petty princes competing with each other, many people claiming that they were kings but they weren't. And we have "Lamentations," a body of literature where people are bemoaning the situation: Oh, things are terrible. We no longer have law and order. Remember, servants are wearing good clothes, and ladies are wearing poor clothes. Things are topsy-turvy. Divine order has been upset.

Well, don't be depressed. Egypt will be okay. Egypt always rises out of it. After this First Intermediate Period we have what we call the Middle Kingdom—prosperity. Life is going to be good, though it's not going to be easy at first, and what we're going to talk about today is one of the two dynasties of the Middle Kingdom. There are only two dynasties in the Middle Kingdom, the eleventh and the twelfth, and we'll talk about the eleventh, which is a kind of desire for unity. We will see kings fighting to sort of pull the country together, and then finally they will get their act together. They'll succeed.

One thing that makes it a little difficult to understand the history of this dynasty for archeologists as well as people who are just interested in Egypt is that the kings all have the same name. The first kings of this dynasty are all named Intef. Now, they have a second name and a third name, but often, often we have fragments of documents, bits of stone, and we just have like "Intef" or maybe "Int," and we know it's one of these kings but we're not sure which one. But the theme to sort of keep in mind is this: The first kings, the Intefs, are not really kings. They are Theban princes, in a sense, who are trying to pull the country together. And then the next set of kings in this dynasty, the Montuhoteps—they all have the same name, too.

They've done it. They've established it. So in the beginning we'll see struggle, and in the end we'll see we've arrived.

First the Intefs. Their names, by the way, are important. If you remember, I said in ancient Egypt names are very important. They have meaning. This is how you can sometimes glean the political situation from a name. For example, our first Intef, Intef Seher-towi—his name means something like "causing the peace in the two lands." *Towi* means "the two lands," Upper and Lower Egypt. So by taking a name like this we can see that he's focused on unity, Upper and Lower Egypt. He writes his name in a cartouche. Now, that's also a bit of optimism. He's saying, "I'm king of Egypt." He's got his name encircled in this magical oval that means he's a king. He's not really. There is not much evidence that he is controlling Upper and Lower Egypt, but at least he's got aspirations. Give him credit.

The next Intef, our second Intef, his name is Wahankh. It's Intef Wahankh. "Ankh," if you remember, means "life." "Wa" means "established," so he's "established in life." The most interesting thing I can tell you about him has nothing to do with his politics and how successful he was. We don't have much of the records from him. He's the first dog lover in history. We have a record, a stela. Remember, they carved those round-topped stones when they wanted to indicate something, leave it for posterity, and we have a stela. It was found by an Egyptologist in 1860, and on this stela are five dogs, his dogs. He just sort of wanted to commemorate that he had these five dogs. He had their names. One was named "Blacky"—kind of neat. So he really liked his dogs. The Egyptians, by the way, were real pet lovers, and it infiltrates into their art.

Let me tell you what to look for when you go to a museum next or when you're looking through art books. When you see a picture, it's usually a tomb painting of a nobleman. When you see him seated on a chair (very common to see the nobility seated on chairs), look underneath the chair. The artist rarely wasted that space. There is almost always going to be something under that chair, and usually it's a pet. You will see a cat, sometimes even a baboon. Sometimes, though, it's not always a pet. Sometimes, if it's a lady, you'll see her cosmetics. You'll see a mirror. She's left a mirror under the chair so she can check out how she looks. But the Egyptians were real pet lovers. Cats were of course top—the number one pet—and then came dogs.

And we have the dog called the whippet, which is really a descendant of the Egyptian pharaoh's hound. It's that kind of dog they had, this thin, wiry dog that looks a little bit like a small greyhound. That was an Egyptian dog. So we know this Intef was a dog lover, and he called himself king of Upper and Lower Egypt. I think it's a bit of a sign of progress that one writes his name in a cartouche and the next one calls himself king of Upper and Lower Egypt.

Now the third Intef—his name is Nakht-neb-tep-nefer, something you can't exactly hum, but it's an important name. *Nakht* means "mighty" or "victorious." *Neb* is usually "lord," means "lord." *Tep* is "front" or "foremost" or something like that, and *nefer* means three things. You have your choice: "good," "beautiful," or "happy." That's why you get a lot of women's names with *nefer* in it, like Nefertiti or Nefertari, "the beautiful one has come." So with *nefer* you always think positively. It's "beautiful," "good," "happy."

So his name means something like "the beautiful and strong champion or lord." So he's really saying he's done it. Now, this is a man that we know really did do it. We know that he went north and fought. These are Theban princes. These are princes from the south, and he went north and actually fought the northerners, so he's really doing something about uniting the country. And he is in a sense the champion that Egypt had been looking for to unite.

That's the end of the Intefs. They've struggled; they've tried to pull it together; they are on the right road. Then come the Montuhoteps. Now, for Montuhotep, the god of war was Montu. So the fact that these kings are taking war god names suggests they are going to battle their way, they are going to fight their way, to unification. Or, if they are not going to fight their way, at least they've seen other people fight their way, and they know you've got to be tough. *Hotep*, of course, means to "be pleased." That's why you get names like Amunhotep: "Amun is pleased."

So Montuhotep means "the war god is pleased," and our first Montuhotep is Montuhotep Se-Ankh-ib-towi. Now, *ib* means "heart," and *towi* we've heard before, "the two lands." So it's something like "causing the heart of the two lands to live," something like that, or maybe even "he gives life to the heart of the two lands." But the idea is that he is the unifier. He's saying, the two lands live in me, and it's true. He really is a king of Upper and Lower Egypt in the full sense of the meaning of it.

Now, what do we know about him? There we start to get a picture of a man. First, he's got resources. He's got money. The reason we know this—we don't have his bank account; we don't have listings of how much he had—is he builds a mortuary temple that is spectacular. A mortuary temple was where the priests would go and pray for him after he was dead. You had to make offerings to the deceased. He didn't know when he was going to resurrect and go in the next world.

So you needed a large facility where people could come and pay their respects and make offerings, and he built a mortuary temple that was spectacular. It's terribly ruined today, but he selected a spot called Deir el Bahri. Now, you've probably heard of this in connection with other things. Hatshepsut would build a wonderful temple there, but when he built there it was pretty desolate. It's on the west side of Thebes, the west side where the dead were buried, so it's a mortuary temple for the dead, and he chooses a spot right against the cliffs. It's a rather stark place. It's white, glistening white. There is nothing growing there. You get these huge cliffs coming up, and right at the foot of the cliffs he builds his mortuary temple, and it's a new kind of monument. It was revolutionary.

In the middle of it is a small pyramid on a kind of platform, and around the pyramid is what we call an ambulatory, a place where you could walk. It was colonnaded, and you could walk. It's rather striking, and it took quite a bit of resources to build something like that. This monument has been excavated many times, and almost every time they excavate it they find something new.

The first excavator was a man named Édouard Naville, and he was excavating just at the turn of the century. In the mortuary temple, right in the mortuary temple, beneath the paving stones, he found the burials of princesses, ladies of the harem of Montuhotep. Then a little bit later, about 20 years later, Herbert Winlock, an excavator for the Metropolitan Museum of Art, began excavating there again. Now, you may wonder, Why excavate when somebody else has already excavated it? Well the answer is, if you know something that the other excavator didn't know, you think you're going to find something, and that's what Winlock did. Winlock figured this way: He looked at the plans and saw there were shrines in the back, and he realized there should be a couple more coffins, a couple more burials for ladies of the harem, and he looked, and he found them.

Interestingly, one of the ladies of the harem, her name was "Maut." Her name really means "kitty," as in "cat," a diminutive of "cat." The ancient Egyptian word for cat was *mau*, as in "meow." It was onomatopoeic. The Egyptians loved words that were onomatopoeic. For example, "cat" was *mau*, one of the words of "cat." "Donkey" was e*a-ah*. And the ancient Egyptian word for wine, I think, is onomatopoeic. It's *irp*, and I think it's like a burp. The Egyptians loved that. So "Kitty" was a lady of the harem, and Winlock found her coffin. He found her intact, virtually. This lady of the harem was five years old. She was a little girl. So she was probably a daughter rather than a lady of the harem. She was really, I guess we could call her, a palace kid. She was one of the kids in the palace.

You can learn a lot, by the way, from just a burial like this. The coffin of Maut is an interesting coffin. It's rectangular, real rectangular. On it is a simple band of hieroglyphs on the outside with two eyes painted on it. I think everyone who sees it says it's elegant. It's a simple rectangle made out of wood. That, by the way, is typical of Middle Kingdom coffins. So you can tell your coffins when you see them. If you see a simple box looking very much like a cedar chest—Middle Kingdom.

It's later in the New Kingdom that you will get the stylized anthropoid coffin shaped like a mummy. That's New Kingdom. We don't have them yet. So a wooden box is Middle Kingdom, with a simple band of hieroglyphs, magical prayer, usually, and on the side are usually two eyes. There are two eyes painted on the side of the coffin so the deceased can look out. Almost always Middle Kingdom burials are on their side so they can look out the side of the coffin, facing west. They know where they are going.

So "Kitty's" coffin tells us something, but there's also another development, and you'll see, it doesn't just happen. There are reasons for these things. In the Middle Kingdom, inside of coffins, we start to get magical spells. The entire inside of coffins are covered with magical spells to help the deceased get to the next world. Why does this appear in the Middle Kingdom? Why now? The answer is one lecture back: the First Intermediate Period.

This is what happened, almost certainly. If you remember, in the Old Kingdom the pharaohs were building pyramids, and we had Unas, the last king of Dynasty V, decide to put Pyramid Texts in his pyramid, magical spells in the burial chamber to help him resurrect in the next world. That's a new development in Dynasty V, Old Kingdom. After him the kings of the Sixth Dynasty thought it was a good idea, and they followed through and had what we call the Pyramid Texts in their pyramids.

But now what happens? Well, the pyramids, of course, are sealed and the pharaohs put inside. The commoner never has an idea of what's inside that pyramid. But then comes the First Intermediate Period and lawlessness. No one is guarding the pyramids. This is when all the pyramids of Egypt were robbed, during the First Intermediate Period. That's when they break into the Great Pyramid at Giza. That's when they rob Sneferu's pyramid. That's when they go into the pyramids of the Fifth and Sixth Dynasties and see Pyramid Texts. Commoners have now seen magical spells that help you resurrect. Wouldn't you want them? Wouldn't you want to resurrect?

The pharaoh had this magical spell. Maybe if you have this magical spell you can resurrect. So if you don't have a pyramid, where are you going to put the magical spell? Inside your coffin. You've got a coffin—you put it inside your coffin. So in the Middle Kingdom, because people saw these spells in the First Intermediate Period and wanted them, they start writing the Pyramid Texts on the insides of their coffins, and we call them the Coffin Texts. So it's a logical evolution. It doesn't just happen. But "Kitty's" rectangular coffin is an example of a typical Middle Kingdom coffin.

Now, back to Montuhotep, our great king of Dynasty XI. To some extent the history of this dynasty is tied to one excavator, Herbert Winlock from the Metropolitan Museum of Art, who excavated there during the 1920s and a little before. Winlock made a discovery that surprised even him one year, and it shows that Montuhotep, I think, really did go to war and fight. The tombs of the nobility of this dynasty—not the kings but the nobility—are around Montuhotep's mortuary temple, cut into the rock. The idea was that the king, when he went to the next world, would be surrounded by his nobility, too, so everybody could go. So there are many little rock-cut tombs near this mortuary temple at Deir el Bahri.

In one of them Winlock found piles of mummies, piles of them, more than 60. At first Winlock thought they were a later burial, somebody reusing a tomb, maybe even in the Coptic period, is what he thought. That is in the first couple of centuries A.D. But when he looked at the mummies carefully, he noticed that on the bandages were names of the deceased, and they were Middle Kingdom names. They were names that are typical of the Middle Kingdom. That was curious. Then Winlock realized they were all males. It was kind of funny that they would be all males in a communal tomb. Women were mummified and buried.

He sent many of the bodies to Douglas Derry, who is an anatomist working at the university in Cairo, to examine them. And Derry said, not only are they all males, they are all in the prime of life. They are all young men. And then Derry saw very clearly that several of them had arrows in them. These were the soldiers of Montuhotep who had gone perhaps north to fight, and their bodies had been brought back for burial near their king's tomb, so Montuhotep really did go out and do some battling.

Interestingly, by the way, you can see one of these mummies or part of it, just a part of it, at the Metropolitan Museum of Art. The Metropolitan exhibits virtually everything they have, everything. There is nothing in the basement. There are little side study rooms where the minor things are, and if you go to the Middle Kingdom section, in the study room on a top shelf on the right-hand corner you will see a shoulder, just a shoulder, of a person. And if you look closely—it's not carefully labeled—there is an arrow in that soldier. That's one of Montuhotep's soldiers. Montuhotep did do some battling.

Winlock continued to excavate in this area, and he made important discoveries, and one I want to use as an example of how excavators aren't always looking for objects. They are not looking for objects all the time. They are looking for knowledge all the time. There was a large tomb in the area, the tomb of Meket-re, who had been the chancellor of Montuhotep. It had been excavated, thoroughly excavated. There was no chance of finding anything. But Winlock had a few extra days and a couple of workmen, and he decided he would clear the tomb completely so that he could measure it accurately, so that he could map it, just so he would have an architectural record of the tomb, wanting nothing more than the knowledge of it.

They had just about cleared the tomb so they could do the measuring when a sharp-eyed workman—and usually, by the way, the local Egyptian workmen that we hire are very skilled. They know what they are doing. They know what they are looking for—as he was sweeping out the sand he saw that some of the sand was disappearing into a crack in the floor of the tomb. He knew that probably meant there was something beneath, maybe another tomb, maybe just a hole in the rock, but he called Winlock, and they discovered an intact chamber, a little chamber with funerary models.

Now, let me explain what these are. In the Middle Kingdom, when you went to the next world, you wanted to have your servants with you. You wanted all the comforts of life, and you had made for you little models of the kinds of amenities and the servants you had in the previous world. So, for example, Meket-re, this wealthy man who would have had estates (he was the chancellor of the king), he had almost like dollhouses, little dioramas. They're maybe three feet square—little, carved, wooden figures. He had a butcher shop, and you can see the men slaughtering the cattle and the meat hanging up to dry.

There was a bakery and a brewery, always next to each other, by the way, in Egypt, because of the yeast. Wherever you find a bakery you'll find a brewery next door always in Egypt. So when excavators find the large vats for the brewery they look for the bakery. And he even had a model of his house. There were servant girls carrying produce back from the market—beautiful things, really beautiful. But Winlock wasn't looking for treasure. He was just looking to map this thing.

The models today are in two museums. People often ask about this. Do you get to keep the stuff you find? Today the answer is, no, we really excavate just for knowledge, and the only thing you keep are your records. Everything stays in Egypt, everything. But in Winlock's day it was 50/50. It was a division of the finds. The excavator took half back to his institution, if it was a university or a museum, and the Egyptian government kept the other half. So half of these models are in the Metropolitan Museum of Art in New York, where Winlock worked, and the other half are in the Egyptian Museum in Cairo, and you can see them. They are really quite, quite lovely things. That's one of the great finds of Winlock. Winlock found many, many things of this period.

Let me tell you one last kind of great, well, there are two more great finds he really did. One is the tomb of Wah. After Meket-re's tomb, he found another intact tomb, an employee of Meket-re, a guy named Wah, which means "established." He was established; he was pretty happy with himself. Wah had an interesting bit of jewelry on his neck. He was buried with a silver scarab, which was to help him exist in the next world. It's a carved beetle, or in this case it's a molded beetle out of silver. When they buried Wah they ritually killed the beetle. In other words, they took the silver amulet, and they hacked out the eyes and the mouth so it couldn't by magic come to life and damage Wah—a little bit of ritual killing.

But anyway, let me tell you a little bit about one Middle Kingdom discovery of Winlock, and you'll see sometimes the history of a dynasty is really one excavator's work. Winlock found a bunch of letters written by a name called Heka Nakht. Now, Heka Nakht had an interesting job. He was a *ka* priest. Remember, the ancient Egyptians believed that the soul was made up of different parts. You were a *ba*, which was your personality, and it was usually shown in the form of a bird with the head of the deceased, so it's a human-headed bird. And the *ba* could kind of flit around while you were lying in your tomb waiting to be resurrected. That was your personality.

There was also the *ka*, which was your double, kind of like your shape, your spiritual shape, and when you died priests had to make offerings to your *ka* because the *ka* needed sustenance, too, had to eat. If you were wealthy enough you would hire somebody forever. You know he's not going to last forever, but you have his family. You would leave an endowment, and the deal is, you get this land. You come to my tomb once a day (on holidays you might have to stay for two days), and make the offerings for my soul. So you would make a deal with a priest: And when you die, or, if you're getting old, your son can take over. You still keep the land and forever make sure that my ka will get its bread and beer in the next world.

Well, Heka Nakht was that kind of priest. He was a *ka* priest. And *ka* priests very often would have to almost live in a tomb a couple of days because you had to make the offerings. He was a *ka* priest for a man named Ip, and sometimes he would have to sleep overnight, and he slept in a neighboring tomb, a smaller tomb. Now, Winlock, when he excavated that small tomb, found the equivalent of an ancient Egyptian wastebasket. Dug in a corner of the tomb was a little pit out of the dirt. When Heka Nakht would come to the tomb and have to spend a lot of time there, he would write letters, and he would take his correspondence with him, letters that he had gotten, and he would write back to his family. From these letters, he would draft rough drafts, maybe, and then he would write it formally.

And from the things that he threw away in the tomb and sort of buried in his wastebasket (he would just drop them in there and cover them with dirt), we learn a little bit about Heka Nakht. He was a very garrulous guy. He was always writing to his sons on his estate and sort of micromanaging everything, telling them, pay this amount of grain for this kind of cattle, and he would always end his letters with "and make sure my concubine isn't mistreated." So he's always giving instructions to his sons. But Winlock found these letters. They are called the Heka Nakht letters today, and because he excavated them they are at the Metropolitan Museum of Art in New York. You can go see them.

But what's really neat about these letters is that Agatha Christie—whose husband was an archeologist, a Near Eastern archeologist, Sir Max Mallowan—she knows Egyptology, and she based a novel on these Heka Nakht letters. And it's not the one you might think, *Death on the Nile*. That's set in modern time. It's called *Death Comes as the End*, and it's quite accurately based on the Heka Nakht letters, and I think you will all enjoy it.

So Winlock helped us uncover the history of Montuhotep. If you look at statues of Montuhotep, though, there is an interesting thing to be learned from them. Montuhotep had wealth. He was established, and his statues of himself show a kind of powerful man. They indicate power. But, they are not well made. They are kind of crude, and I think the reason they are crude is that, during the First Intermediate Period, the royal sculptors, the royal studios where royal art was cranked out, were no longer supported. There was no king who had a royal studio. So, in a sense, while he had the means, he had lost the skills, or at least the sculptors had lost the skills to really produce fine art. So that's an interesting trait in the beginning of the Middle Kingdom. They'll get it back. They'll get it back, but not yet. They are not yet there.

Now, what about Montuhotep's successors? There are some Montuhoteps following him. His successor is Montuhotep Se-Ankh-Ka-Re, "causing the *ka* of 'Re' to live." *Ka* is the soul, and "Re" is the god, "causing the soul of 'Re' to live." He succeeded his father, a sign that things are going well. There is stability—the son succeeds the father. He sent an expedition to the Wadi Hammamat. The Wadi Hammamat is an ancient caravan route. It had been used for thousands of years. Just outside of Thebes it starts and goes to the Red Sea, through desert. It's treacherous, not easy. It's not easy by any means.

But the reason Egyptians wanted to go to the Wadi Hammamat is that it was a source of fine, black stone. The kind of stone that you see sometimes in sarcophagi, these black sarcophagi, almost always comes from the Wadi Hammamat. He sent an expedition there of 3,000 men. That's a sign that you're established. Three thousand men going there wasn't easy, and the overseer of these men even records, we dug twelve wells along the way so the men would be okay. They even have little details, you know, the men who kept the record of these expeditions. This was something you would remember for the rest of your life. So these guys have things like "I supplied two pots of water for every man on a pole that they carried on their shoulders." Or "they had donkey loads of sandals because the sandals were wearing out from marching." So it's quite a good thing to be able to send an expedition to the Wadi Hammamat. This is a dynasty that is established.

Now, his successor, another Montuhotep, Neb-towi-Re—which means something like "'Re' is lord of the two lands; they are unified"—he also sends a Wadi Hammamat expedition, this one of 10,000. Big. Imagine all the sculptors, the chisel men, the men who were going to take care of the tools. And there is one little detail about this expedition that's quite something. They were looking for a stone that was just right for the sarcophagus of the pharaoh, and when they arrived a pregnant gazelle came in front of them, and they followed this pregnant gazelle, and she gave birth on a stone that was just right for the pharaoh. Unfortunately, the record also says they sacrificed the gazelle because they thought this was a great sign.

But this is a dynasty that can build large temples. They can send expeditions to the Wadi Hammamat. They can bury their princesses in nice coffins with jewelry. This is Egypt reestablished. It's only one of two dynasties in the Middle Kingdom. Next time we'll talk about the next dynasty. See you then.

Classical Egyptian Alphabet

Hieroglyph	Description	Sound
	vulture	a
	foot	b
	placenta	ch
	hand	d
	arm	e
	horned viper	f
	jar stand	g
	twisted flax	h
	reed leaf	i
	snake	j(dj)
	basket	k

Classical Egyptian Alphabet

Hieroglyph	Description	Sound
owl image	owl	m
water image	water	n
mat image	mat	p
hill image	hill	q
mouth image	mouth	r
folded cloth image	folded cloth	s
pool of water image	pool of water	sh
loaf of bread image	loaf of bread	t
tethering ring image	tethering ring	tch
quail chick image	quail chick	u / w
two reed leaves image	two reed leaves	y
door bolt image	door bolt	z

Timeline

Glossary

Archaising: An artistic or literary style that imitates techniques of the Old Kingdom.

Ba: Part of the soul, usually represented as having the head of a man and the body of a bird.

Ben-ben stone: The earliest form of the obelisk, worshipped in temples.

Book of the Dead: A collection of magical spells and prayers intended to help the deceased resurrect in the next world.

Canopic jars: Four jars used to hold the internal organs removed at the time of mummification.

Cartouche: An oval encircling the name of a king or queen.

Cenotaph: A symbolic tomb in addition to the deceased's real place of burial.

Coptic: Christian art and religion as practiced in Egypt.

Corbel: An inward stepping of the walls of a room toward the ceiling.

Coregency: Two pharaohs ruling at the same time by agreement, usually father and son.

Demotic: A later form of writing the Egyptian language used after the seventh century B.C. The word is from the Greek meaning *people*, because it was the secular form of writing, as opposed to hieroglyphs.

Determinative hieroglyph: A hieroglyph placed at the end of a word to clarify its meaning.

Faience: A ceramic material used for making amulets and tiles.

Festival of Opet: A religious festival during which the statues of the gods Amun, Mut, and Khonsu were taken from Karnak Temple to Luxor Temple.

Heb-sed festival: A ritual intended to be celebrated every thirty years by the pharaoh to ensure his rejuvenation.

Hieratic: The cursive form of writing the Egyptian language derived from hieroglyphs.

Hypostyle hall: A room of a temple with columns supporting a roof.

Ka: Part of the deceased's soul that is thought of as a double.

Kings list: An official list of the kings of Egypt, usually carved on a temple wall.

Kiosk: A small, open structure made of stone, usually attached to a temple in honor of a god.

Maat: Divine order; also, the Goddess of Truth.

Mastaba: A bench-shaped structure above a tomb, especially during the Old Kingdom.

Mummy: Any preserved cadaver.

Natron: A naturally occurring mixture of sodium carbonate, sodium bicarbonate, and sodium chloride—used to dehydrate the body in mummification.

Necrotome: A knife believed to have been used by embalmers ("death knife").

Obelisk: A tall shaft of a single stone, usually pink granite. Obelisks were placed in pairs at the entrances to temples.

Oracle: A person divinely inspired who foresees the future.

Papyrus: Writing material made from the stalks of the papyrus plant.

Pharaoh: The divine ruler of Egypt, associated with Horus, the falcon god.

Pylon: A monumental gateway or entrance to a temple or palace.

Registration: In art works, the practice of having different figures on different levels or registers.

Relieving chambers: Small rooms designed to distribute the weight stresses of the pyramid above; also called "stress-relieving chambers."

Resurrection: The belief that the body will get up and live again in the next world.

Sarcophagus: A stone receptacle for preserving a mummy.

Scarab: The sacred beetle. Often amulets were carved in this shape to ensure continued existence.

Serekh: A schematic representation of a palace facade with a rectangle above it in which the king's Horus name was written.

Sesperonch: A Coptic word for "magician" derived from the ancient Egyptian words "scribe of the house of life."

Stela: A round-topped standing stone carved with an inscription.

Stretching the Cord: A ceremony performed at the beginning of the construction of a temple.

Ushabti: Small statues of servants intended to serve the deceased in the next world.

Bibliography

General History and Chronology

Aldred, Cyril. *The Egyptians*. London: Thames & Hudson, 1998. A concise overview by a noted Egyptologist.

Breasted, James Henry. *A History of Egypt*. New York: Scribner's, 1920. Amazingly, this is still one of the most readable histories of Egypt and is still mostly accurate.

Clayton, Peter. *Chronicle of the Pharaohs*. London: Thames and Hudson, 1994. A wonderful dynasty-by-dynasty illustrated history of Egypt.

Dodson, Aidan. *Monarchs of the Nile*. London: Rubicon Press, 1995. Brief descriptions of each pharaoh's reign. More a reference work than a readable history.

Gardiner, Alan. *Egypt of the Pharaohs*. Oxford: Oxford University Press, 1972. A dated work but by a great authority who gives many interesting details based on linguistic research. Not an easy read.

Hoffman, Michael A. *Egypt Before the Pharaohs*. New York: Knopf, 1979. The best book on prehistoric Egypt.

James, T. G. H. *An Introduction to Ancient Egypt*. New York: Farrar, Straus & Giraux, 1979. A concise and accurate history by the former Keeper of Egyptian Antiquities of the British Museum.

Mertz, Barbara. *Temples, Tombs, and Hieroglyphs*. New York: Dodd, Mead & Co., 1978. The first popular book on Egyptology by an Egyptologist and still the most entertaining. The author is also known as Elizabeth Peters and writes murder mysteries set in Egypt.

———. *Red Land, Black Land*. New York: Dodd, Mead & Co., 1978. The sequel to the above. Not a chronological history of Egypt, but it covers the high points.

Rice, Michael. *Egypt's Making*. London: Routledge, 1995. Detailed, authoritative telling of Egypt's early history from 5000–2000 B.C. Well illustrated.

Winlock, H. E. *The Rise and Fall of the Middle Kingdom in Thebes*. New York: Macmillan, 1947. An old work, so some of the details are wrong, but gives the best feeling for the period.

Art

Aldred, Cyril. *The Development of Ancient Egyptian Art.* London: Tiranti, 1965. An old standard combining three of the author's smaller works: *Old Kingdom, Middle Kingdom,* and *New Kingdom Art in Ancient Egypt.*

Bothmer, Bernard. *Egyptian Sculpture of the Late Period.* New York: The Brooklyn Museum, 1960. An exhibition catalog but also a standard work on the subject. Some of the pieces have recently been attributed to different dates, but the book is still an essential reference.

Kischkewitz, Hannelore. *Egyptian Art: Drawings and Paintings.* London: Hamlyn, 1989. Detailed discussions of how ancient artists produced Books of the Dead and tomb paintings.

―――. *Egyptian Drawings.* London: Octopus, 1972. Covers much that is in the work above but does not provide as much detail.

Michalowski, Kazimierz. *Art of Ancient Egypt.* New York: Abrams, n.d. The most lavish history of Egyptian art. The illustrations are beautiful and the text important.

―――. *Great Sculpture of Ancient Egypt.* New York: William Morrow, 1978. Excellent photos and brief discussions of masterpieces in the Egyptian Museum in Cairo.

Murray, Margaret Alice. *Egyptian Sculpture.* New York: Scribner's, 1930. A somewhat dated survey but contains a great illustration of a carving by a student of a hand with six fingers!

Peck, William H. *Egyptian Drawing.* London: Thames and Hudson, 1978. Good survey of the subject.

Rachewiltz, Boris de. *Egyptian Art.* New York: Viking, 1960. A good, solid work frequently found in used bookstores.

Russmann, Edna R. *Egyptian Sculpture: Cairo and Luxor.* Austin: University of Texas Press, 1989. Discussions of important pieces of sculpture. The text is by a great authority on the subject.

Scamuzzi, Ernesto. *Egyptian Art in the Egyptian Museum of Turin.* New York: Abrams, n.d. Presentation of a wonderful collection rarely seen by Americans.

Westendorf, Wolfhart. *Painting, Sculpture, and Architecture of Ancient Egypt.* New York: Abrams, 1968. Standard work with good illustrations. Frequently found in used bookstores.

Woldering, Imgard. *The Art of Ancient Egypt*. New York: Greystone Press, 1962. A good survey, strong on details of how art was produced.

Building and the Pyramids

Arnold, Dieter. *Building in Egypt*. Oxford: Oxford University Press, 1991. The definitive work and a great read.

Edwards, I. E. S. *The Pyramids of Egypt*. New York: Viking, 1985. An older work but still the best on the subject.

Fakhry, Ahmed. *The Pyramids*. Chicago: University of Chicago Press, 1969. A solid work by the Egyptian authority on the pyramids.

Habachi, Labib. *The Obelisks of Egypt*. New York: Scribner's, 1977. The best popular account of obelisks.

Lehner, Mark. *The Complete Pyramids*. London: Thames & Hudson, 1997. Written by a real expert, this volume has wonderful computer-generated illustrations.

Mendelssohn, Kurt. *The Riddle of the Pyramids*. New York: Praeger, 1974. Interesting reading, but the theory presented is probably false.

Noakes, Aubrey. *Cleopatra's Needles*. London: Wicherby, 1962. A popular account of the modern moving of obelisks.

Tompkins, Peter. *Secrets of the Great Pyramid*. New York: Harper & Row, 1971. Good for illustrations and occult theories on the pyramid, but not much else.

Hieroglyphs

Collier, Mark, and Bill Manley. *How to Read Egyptian Hieroglyphs*. Berkeley: University of California Press, 1998. One of the best brief treatments that helps you learn by yourself.

Fischer, Henry. *Ancient Egyptian Calligraphy*. New York: Metropolitan Museum of Art, 1979. Delightful book that shows you how to draw the hieroglyphs. Great therapy!

Gardiner, Alan. *Egyptian Grammar*. Oxford: Griffith Institute, 1957. Still the definitive work; large, not easy to use by yourself, but wonderful.

Quirke, Stephen, and Carol Andrews. *The Rosetta Stone*. London: British Museum, 1988. Everything you want to know intelligently presented.

Kings and Queens

Arrian. *The Campaigns of Alexander the Great.* New York: Dorset, 1971. A primary source.

Bevan, Edwyn R. *The House of Ptolemy.* Chicago: Ares, reprint (original 1927), republished in 1968. An important source of information on the period and the Ptolemies.

Bianchi, Robert. *Cleopatra's Egypt.* New York: Brooklyn Museum, 1988. Spectacular exhibition catalogue of art from the time of Cleopatra. Also includes much useful historical information.

Bradford, Ernle. *Cleopatra.* New York: Harcourt Brace, 1972. A detailed but readable biography.

Brier, Bob. *The Murder of Tutankhamen.* New York: Putnam's, 1998. Theory that the boy-king was killed but also presents historical background.

Desmond, Alice Curtis. *Cleopatra's Children.* New York: Dodd, 1971. The only work on what happened to Cleo's kids. Readable and well researched.

Foreman, Laura. *Cleopatra's Palace.* New York: Random House, 1999. A beautiful book tied to a television special but better than the program.

Fox, Robin Lane. *Alexander the Great.* New York: Dial, 1974. A readable, accurate biography.

Freed, Rita A. *Ramses the Great.* Boston: Boston Museum of Science, 1987. An exhibition catalogue but with a concise history of Ramses and good photographs of objects from the period.

George, Margaret. *Memoirs of Cleopatra.* New York: St. Martin's Press, 1997. A monumental, historically accurate fictional biography of Cleopatra. Wonderful.

Grant, Michael. *Cleopatra.* New York: Simon and Schuster, 1972. Solid biography of the last queen of Egypt.

————. *From Alexander to Cleopatra.* New York: Scribner's, 1982. Rich background to the lives of the kings and queens of the Greek period.

Hughes-Hallett, Lucy. *Cleopatra.* New York, Harper, 1990. More a social history of how Cleopatra was viewed than a biography. Quite interesting.

Kitchen, K. A. *Pharaoh Triumphant: The Life and Times of Ramses II*. Cairo: American University in Cairo Press, 1982. The definitive work by the leading Ramses scholar. Highly readable.

Lindsay, Jack. *Cleopatra*. New York: Coward McCann, 1970. Readable, literary type of biography, sans footnotes.

Tyldesley, Joyce. *Hatchepsut*. New York: Viking, 1996. The most recent and best biography of the female pharaoh.

Medicine

Breasted, James Henry. *The Edwin Smith Surgical Papyrus*. Chicago: University of Chicago Press, 1930. Hieroglyphs and translation of a papyrus that told physicians how to treat trauma. Fascinating.

Bryan, Cyril P. *Ancient Egyptian Medicine—Papyrus Ebers*. Chicago: Ares, 1974. Translation of a papyrus that includes magical/pharmacological treatments for many ailments.

Estes, J. Worth. *The Medical Skills of Ancient Egypt*. Canton: Science History Publications, 1993. Useful.

Ghalioungui, Paul. *The House of Life*. Amsterdam: Ben Israel, 1973. Written by an Egyptologist/physician, this is one of the best overviews of the medical practice in ancient Egypt.

Nunn, John F. *Ancient Egyptian Medicine*. London: British Museum, 1996. The most recent and best work on the subject. Illustrated.

Mummies

Brier, Bob. *Egyptian Mummies*. New York: William Morrow, 1994. The basic survey of the subject.

Budge, E. A. Wallis. *The Mummy*. New York: Causeway, 1974. Reprint of a 100-year-old classic. Much is outdated but good for hieroglyphic spells associated with mummification.

Cockburn, Aidan, et al. *Mummies, Disease and Ancient Cultures*. Cambridge: Cambridge University Press, 1998. Mummies around the world but much on Egypt, focusing on high-tech paleopathology.

El Mahdy, Christine. *Mummies, Myth and Magic*. London: Thames & Hudson, 1989. Popular survey with interesting illustrations but too many errors to be trusted.

Ikram, Salima, and Aidan Dodson. *The Mummy in Ancient Egypt.* London: Thames & Hudson, 1998. Wonderfully illustrated survey of funerary practices. Much on coffins, canopic chests, and so on.

Partridge, Robert B. *Faces of Pharaohs.* London: Rubicon, 1994. Photos of all the royal mummies and their coffins with brief descriptions. Useful for reference.

Pettigrew, Thomas J. *A History of Egyptian Mummies.* Los Angeles: North American Archives, n.d. Reprint of 1834 work by the greatest mummy unroller of all times. Gives many references of ancient comments on mummification.

Smith, G. Elliot, and Warren R. Dawson. *Egyptian Mummies.* London: Kegan Paul, 1991. Reprint of the 1924 work that was the basic book on the subject for years. Still useful.

Religion

Frankfort, H. *Ancient Egyptian Religion.* New York: Columbia University Press, 1948. A fundamental work on the topic but very dated.

Hornung, Erick. *Conceptions of God in Ancient Egypt.* Ithaca: Cornell University Press, 1985. Excellent essays but a bit technical.

Morentz, Sigfried. *Egyptian Religion.* Ithaca: Cornell University Press, 1973. A solid work.

Akhenaten and the Amarna Period

Aldred, Cyril. *Akhenaten, King of Egypt.* London: Thames & Hudson, 1988. One of the two or three basic works on the subject by a highly respected Amarna scholar.

―――. *Akhenaten and Nefertiti.* New York: Brooklyn Museum, 1973. An exhibition catalogue that includes important information on the subject.

Anon. *Amarna Letters*, 3 vols. San Francisco: KMT Communications, 1991–1994. Anthologies of essays by various scholars. Both readable and informative.

Arnold, Dorothea. *The Royal Women of Amarna.* New York: Metropolitan Museum of Art, 1997. Essays by various scholars on the different women of the Amarna period. Beautiful illustrations, important text.

Desroches-Noblecourt, Christiane. *Tutankhamen*. New York: New York Graphic Society, 1963. Some unusual theories but gives a wonderful feeling of the period.

Kozloff, Arielle P., and Betsy M. Bryan. *Egypt's Dazzling Sun*. A beautifully illustrated exhibition catalogue but far more, including the best history of Amenhotep III available.

Moran, William. *The Amarna Letters*. Baltimore: Johns Hopkins University Press, 1992. Translations of the cuneiform letters written to Akhenaten from abroad. Shows Egypt declining.

Murnane, William J. *Texts from the Amarna Period in Egypt*. Atlanta: Scholars Press, 1995. Translations of all the major Egyptian documents from the period. An important research tool and fascinating.

————, and Charles C. Van Siclen III. *The Boundary Stelae of Akhenaten*. London: Kegan-Paul, 1993. Translations of all the boundary markers of Akhenaten's city in the desert.

Redford, D. B. *Akhenaten, the Heretic King*. Princeton: Princeton University Press, 1984. An important work by the man who excavated Akhenaten's temples at Karnak and grew to hate the king!

Reeves, Nicholas. *The Complete Tutankhamen*. London: Thames & Hudson, 1990. It really is complete! (With wonderful illustrations.)

————, and John H. Taylor. *Howard Carter Before Tutankhamen*. New York: Abrams, 1992. Gives a detailed account of Carter's career leading up to the discovery of Tutankhamen's tomb.

Smith, Ray Winfield, and Donald B. Redford. *The Akhenaten Temple Project*. Warminster: Aris & Phillips, 1976. The attempt to reconstruct Akhenaten's Karnak temples on paper with the aid of a computer.

Velikovsky, Immannuel. *Oedipus and Akhenaten*. New York: Doubleday, 1960. A crazy theory that Akhenaten was the Greek King Oedipus, but it is interesting to see how the case is presented.

Daily Life

Erman, Adolf. *Life in Ancient Egypt*. New York: Dover, 1971. Reprint of a 100-year-old work but still useful for its illustrations of the details of the lives of the ancient Egyptians.

Maspero, Gaston C. C. *Life in Ancient Egypt and Assyria*. New York: Unger, 1971. Reprint of a 100-year-old work but useful.

Wilkinson, J. Gardner. *The Ancient Egyptians: Their Lives and Customs*. New York: Crescent Books, 1988. Reprint of a 100-year-old work that is dated in some of its conclusions but includes hundreds of wonderful line drawings from the tombs of the nobles at Thebes.

Miscellaneous

Bietak, Manfred. *Avaris, The Capital of the Hyksos*. London: British Museum, 1996. Excavation report that shows how difficult it is to reconstruct the history of the Hyksos.

Brier, Bob. *Ancient Egyptian Magic*. New York: Morrow, 1980. A broad survey of magical practices.

————. *The Glory of Ancient Egypt*. Millwood: Kraus Reprint Co., 1988. Much information on Napoleon's Egyptian campaign and the *Description de l'Egypte*.

Budge, Wallis. *Egyptian Magic*. New York: University Books, n.d. Reprint of an 1899 work but still contains some useful information.

Frerichs, Ernest, and Leonard Lesko. *Exodus, the Egyptian Evidence*. Winona Lake: Eisenbrauns, 1997. A small book of essays by experts on both sides of the Exodus question.

Herold, J. Christopher. *Bonaparte in Egypt*. New York: Harper, 1962. The author hates Bonaparte, but the book is a wonderful read with great information.

Sandars, N. K. *The Sea Peoples*. London: Thames & Hudson, 1978. One of the few books on this important subject.

Societies

The Amarna Research Foundation, Inc., 6082 E. Loyola Place, Aurora, CO 80013. Interested in all aspects of the Amarna period, the foundation's activities center on the current excavations at Amarna headed by Dr. Barry Kemp. A newsletter is published.

American Research Center in Egypt (ARCE), Emory University, West Campus, 1256 Briarcliff Road, NE, Building A, Suite 423W, Atlanta, Georgia, 30306. Organization of professional Egyptologists and laymen interested in all aspects of Egypt, including Coptic and Islamic. An annual conference is held and a journal (*JARCE*) is published. The following chapters sponsor lectures by Egyptologists and publish newsletters.

- North Texas Chapter: P.O. Box 38642, Dallas, TX 57238

- Southern California Chapter: 3460 South Broadway, Los Angeles, CA 90007.

- Northern California Chapter: P.O. Box 11352, Berkeley, CA, 94712.

- Washington, D.C. Chapter: 3737 Fessenden Street NW, Washington, D.C., 20016.

Ancient Egypt Studies Association (AESA), 7110 S.E. 29th Avenue, Portland, Oregon, 97202. A group of interested laypersons and professionals with regular meetings, lectures, and a newsletter.

Egypt Exploration Society (EES), 3 Doughty Mews, London WC1N 2PG, London, England. Publishes the *Journal of Egyptian Archaeology*, as well as a glossy magazine, *Egyptian Archaeology*, and sponsors several lectures in London each year.

Egyptian Study Society (ESS), Denver Museum of Natural History, 2001 Colorado Boulevard, Denver, CO, 80205. Another group of interested laypersons and professionals with meetings, lectures, and a newsletter.

Egyptological Seminar of New York (ESNY), P.O. Box 1451, Cooper Station, NY, NY 10276. Sponsors lectures in New York by visiting Egyptologists and publishes a journal, *Bulletin of the Egyptological Seminar of New York (BES)*, and a newsletter.

KMT: A Modern Journal of Ancient Egypt, Dept. G, P.O. Box 1475, Sebastopol, CA 95473. The journal publishes articles on culture, history, personalities, arts, and monuments of ancient Egypt.

Oriental Institute, University of Chicago, 1155 East 58 St., Chicago, IL 60637. Sponsors lectures in Chicago and programs for children and has a correspondence course in hieroglyphs. A newsletter is published, as well as an annual report of the Institute's activities.